An Ordinary Bab

An Ordinary Baby

Tales of Childhood Resistance

Written and Illustrated by

Micheline Mason

YOUCAXTON
PUBLICATIONS

ISBN 978-1-914424-66-3
Published by YouCaxton Publications 2022
YCBN: 01

YouCaxton Publications
www.youcaxton.co.uk

An Ordinary Baby

Once I was an ordinary baby

Chubby arms

Tiny fingernails

A shock of hair

Someone to be loved

Cuddled and sung to

Bathed and fed

Close to my mother

A bright future ahead

I felt safe

I was an ordinary baby

For four short days

Before the cold table

The huge camera

The radiographer's skill

Revealed my hidden secret

And the world stepped back

Abandoning me

To forces we could not fight

Larger than love

Judgement

A redefining of my value

A bleak future

All delight snuffed out

Like a light

What could I make of this

Left to scream

In my hospital cot

I felt irredeemably flawed

Flailing in space

My future in doubt

My Daddy's eyes saved me

Green and sparkly

The delight came back

As we looked and looked

The connection once made

Could not be broken

The look reminded me

I had once felt safe

And I knew,

Somehow I knew

He would co me back one day

Not just to visit

But to take me home

Micheline

December 2007

“Revolutions begin when those defined
as the problem achieve the power to
redefine the problem”

John McKnight

“I think you should be a writer. I am sure
someone would be interested
in your funny ideas…”

Aline Mason 1967

Contents

Foreward

THE SHIP IS READY to steam off from Port Louis in Mauritius. On board are three sisters and a brother, all setting off to a new life in England, half way across the world. Marcelle, Therese, Peter and the youngest, Aline have all been demobilised from the British Army after their first venture overseas to Palestine, just as the War was finishing. In Palestine they had all succeeded in reaching the goal of escaping from the tiny tropical island where they had lived – to meet the partner of their dreams who would take them away from their frightening father and find a better life with more opportunities overseas. Sadly, the man who had courted Therese was killed in action, but Marcelle had met George, a Major in the British Army and Aline had fallen head over heels in love with a tall dark handsome telegraph operator called Lawrence. Peter too had met Maria, an Italian woman living in England whom he hoped to marry.

Although very young, in their early twenties, they were looking forward to making a better life for themselves in the 'Motherland' and had no intention of ever returning home. They all prayed that their relatively fair skin would enable them to pass as 'white' even though the Army had classified them all as 'Coloured'. They knew that racism was deeply entrenched in Britain as well as Mauritius. The less they said about their heritage the better. It would be OK to speak French in England, but not Creole, their first language, which was the language of the 'blacks'. That would give the game away.

Aline was the ninth child of ten. She was bought up with not enough to eat, playing on the slopes of the volcano and running wild through the sugar cane fields, stealing guavas, mangos and lychees from the farmers before they were chased away.

Her mother, Nounoune, had cleverly found wealthy Godparents for Aline and Marcelle, Godparents who were willing to pay for their education. They went to school in a taxi, but stepped out of it in rags, only to be ridiculed by the children who could really pay for it. Nevertheless, they passed their exams and found jobs in the Police and Education before joining the British Army. They had been posted to Palestine, then under British rule, to work in the Army offices as secretaries and clerical workers.

Now, the War over, Aline was embarking on a three-month voyage to Scotland, in the British Isles where she was hoping, with beating heart, that the man she had met there, who had made all the promises, would be true to his word, waiting for her on the Quayside.

∫

Lawrence Charles Mason had joined the Army at nineteen, unable to read and write. He had grown up in Yorkshire, also knowing what it was like to be poor and hungry. His father was a painter and decorator but unfortunately a dishonest man. The many moves they made as a family were to avoid debt collectors. Lawrence's mother. Edith Hines, decided to become the reliable breadwinner. A great cook, she found a job in the Grosvenor Hotel in London as a 'Chef', unusual in those days, and the family got by. His Dad disappeared.

The poverty of the times led to Lawrence becoming ill with tuberculosis, or 'consumption'. He was sent to an open-air school where he did indeed get better, but did not receive an education. He left school at thirteen, pursuing a series of gruelling apprenticeships in such varied skills as sheet-metal bending and furniture upholstery. Although having no desire to be a soldier, or combatant of any kind, he opted to join the Army at nineteen because he knew once there he would be given the opportunity to complete his education and become literate. He also learned to drive (a skill which was too expensive for many working-class people to acquire in civilian life).

During the War he became a skilled operator of Morse Code. This led to his posting to Palestine as part of the communication service for the British Army. He was there at the time of the terrorist attack on the King David Hotel (1946).

One night, there was a dance, or 'Ball' to which both men and women Army Personnel serving overseas were invited. There he was mesmerised by a young woman with dark wavy hair, a French accent, and a shy manner which captivated him. Her name was Aline. She also was captivated by the green eyes, black hair and tall frame. That night, both lives changed forever.

More than a year later he was indeed waiting for her at the Quayside, as promised.

CHAPTER ONE

My Arrival

MANY PEOPLE WERE WAITING for my arrival into the world. My Dad the fireman, my Mum the Mauritian beauty, my sister, Nanny, Aunts & Uncles. Some had knitted and all had imagined the new, soft, pink squawking baby that would make everyone happy. But I was born awkward. Bottom first. Perhaps the first sign that I was not going to follow any expected path in my life, and consequently I would drag them with me, tied by the bonds of love into a world about which they knew nothing.

I cannot say I remember being born. Presenting the doctors at Kingston Hospital with a breech birth I can only guess at the man-handling which had to be done to get me out and breathing. I am sure there were sighs of relief all round when they succeeded and handed me to my Mum as a fait accompli. I am sure I was glad to be alive and in the loving arms of my family. I was deemed normal with a lusty scream showing that my lungs were working just fine. My family brought the soft blankets, the pretty clothes and the sturdy carrycot and took me home, probably on the bus.

For four days I was an ordinary baby. We lived with my Dad's mother who we called 'Nanny' in her small house in Mortlake, Surrey. Nearly everyone in my huge extended family of 51 first cousins were dark-haired and brown-eyed with the exception of two - one cousin and me who had managed to come out 'fair' with reddish hair and the possibility of freckles.

The thing was that I kept crying every time I was moved. Feeding me, dressing me became a noisy nightmare. "You turned black" my Mum told me, describing the intensity of my distress. Finally, all the adults agreed that something was not right. I seemed to be in constant pain and a momentous decision was made to take me back to the hospital to ask if something was wrong.

X-rays Change My Life

They tell you that babies cannot remember things but this is not true. I remember, as I lay all alone on the huge, cold x-ray table a feeling deep inside me - a fearful conviction that the whole world had stepped back from me. Diagnosis: 'Osteogenesis Imperfecta', or Brittle Bones. The X-ray had shown fractured femurs and other abnormalities. Prognosis - imminent death. This was based on the Doctor's previous experience of losing a baby he had cared-for to internal bleeding caused by multiple fractures of ribs, skull and elsewhere. He deduced that as that baby also had OI, I would be another failure on his part. He didn't seem to know that there are several types of OI, his dead baby having the most severe form whilst I had a considerably less severe form. In his unknowing, he advised my parents to have me baptised as quickly as possible, to leave me in the hospital where I would be cared for properly, by experts, until the inevitable day when I slipped into merciful oblivion and they could get on with their lives.

It is dark, it is vast, it is an empty space with no love left. My value as a human being has been re-defined by the rogue genetic flaw in my ability to make collagen. The other thousands of genes which are also my inheritance are suddenly irrelevant, or invisible. I am condemned without a trial. My parents do not come from the social class who feel they could question the men in white coats, to their faces anyway. I am baptised 'Pro Mortis' (before death) and left in my little incubator, in the ward, in the wing, in the hospital, in the town that is not Home.

But not really. Someone is smiling over the edge of my box. His eyes are green and sparkly and his mouth is upturned. He speaks but I do not understand the words. He communicates something of much greater importance - he is delighted in me. My Daddy has come to visit. Suddenly the sun has come out in my world. OK, if there is one person who can see who I really am, I will hang on. I will hang on between visits. I will hang on until my life goes back to how it was before, when I was still an ordinary baby. I will yell and shout until everyone listens. Maybe this is how the pattern of my life is set.

Things go from bad to worse. I catch German Measles and have to be put in an isolation hospital for several weeks. Now even the bedside visits from the green sparkly eyes, and the worried brown eyes of my mother are banished. They can only look at me through a glass window, trying to smile and catch my attention. This memory was painfully etched into my parent's minds as they told me about it repeatedly when I was older. I hold no personal memory of anything except a feeling of abandonment.

Whilst most babies are fed to the clock in these days, the 1950's, due to the malevolent influence of Dr Spock, it is common practice in hospitals to only feed disabled babies 'on demand'. The attitude underlying this practice is an assumption that death for children with incurable (genetic) conditions would be a merciful release from a lifetime of suffering, and a merciful release for the tax payer who would have to fork out for the cost of a lifetime of care for someone who couldn't contribute anything to the world. Many babies born with conditions such as Down's Syndrome, or who have birth injuries resulting in cerebral palsy, do not automatically suck, or appear hungry, and need coaxing or more help than usual to feed. If they don't wail for help then obviously the baby weakens further and often succumbs to some infection, or literally dies of starvation. Luckily for me I am not one of these quiet, passive babies. I am fed, probably as much to keep me quiet as to keep me alive, so I continue to stay alert and grow.

I am unaware of the difficulties the doctors imagine my parents will face trying to care for this very brittle baby. They have no confidence in my foreign mother's abilities in this area. Much later my Mother tells me that they made her come to live in the hospital to try and train her in nappy-changing techniques and so on. However, whilst the medics are still undecided about whether they should release me into her care, my parents do their own thinking. They think that I really am not so different from their other child Brenda; that I don't like being in hospital; will never get 'better' because there is no treatment that can be given to me, and anyway, I am rather sweet and pretty just as I am, with all that titian hair and possibility of freckles. They decide to take matters into their own hands, and bring me home. The medics consequently give up waiting for my departure to Heaven and, with my parents, begin to plan my departure to Mortlake instead.

I am a very beloved nine-month-old child.

CHAPTER TWO

Memories from Mortlake

AGED THREE, LIKE KERMIT the frog I have a stair upon which I liked to sit, not at the bottom and not at the top. It is the widest stair forming a corner of the short flight leading from the scullery to the longer flight downstairs where my Nanny lives. I am sitting on my stair playing with a wheeled pig which I am rolling on the wooden part of the stair, not covered by the rather rough stair carpet beneath my bottom. "Will you stop rolling that thing and making that horrible noise!" Mum says in an irritated voice. I look up and see her bustling about cooking a meal for us in her tiny, green room which was our 'upstairs kitchen' or scullery. I think my Nanny has a much larger one downstairs.

I like staying near enough to Mum that I can feel her presence, but I also like having a view of the drop between the bannisters to the hall below. This is because I have a favourite game which requires me to sit on the stair not making myself too visible to my victim below or from the spoilsport above in the scullery. I wait until my Nanny comes in the front door, hangs up her hat and coat on the large wooden coat hooks waiting for them on the wall, and starts walking unsuspectingly along the hall to her rooms. I look down at the top of her moving head, take aim and drop something on it. I just love her jumping with surprise and holding her head, looking up and saying "Oow, where did that come from !?" whilst I burst into giggles. Hundreds of little toys and various stolen bits and pieces plummeted down from our landing, bounced on her head and fell to the floor, needing to be retrieved by one of the adults around me. "STOP DOING THIS!" I was endlessly told as they were forced to make yet another journey up and down the stairs. But I understand that Nanny knows it is a game and enjoys my laughter as she plays along.

Barnes Common

We are going for a walk with Daddy. My sister is trotting along as he pushes me in my push-chair up to the top of First Avenue where we live, to the corner where there was a shop selling smelly dead fish which I don't like, and then along the road. At some point on this journey we leave the streets with their houses, shops and cars to cross a wooden bumpy thing which my Dad says is a cattle grid. Both the bumps and the thought of big cows frighten me a bit but not for long. We are now in a different world entirely - the magic of Barnes Common. The sun is out, the sky is blue and the air held the soft aroma of cut grass. It is green, buzzing with insects, lit up by flowers, birds and butterflies all alive and dancing in the breeze. We make our way to a round pond of shimmering water where my sister is helped to sail her little boat. She is allowed to take off her shoes and socks and actually step into the splishy- splashy container of coloured light even though she will get wet.

Wind in the poplar trees

I am beginning to feel jealous but my attention is distracted from this scene by hearing a growing roar and rustle, getting louder and louder with apparently nothing to cause it. I look around to find out where the noise is coming from, left and right, then up to where something is moving. I see the leaves on an enormous poplar tree start to wave and turn over, changing from green to silver as a huge gust of wind travels from the bottom of the tree crashing noisily upwards through its branches to their delicate swaying tips, then vanishing into the sky leaving the marvellous tree all still and quiet, undamaged, just waiting to repeat the drama with the next gust of wind. I look at my Dad with open eyes, "Did you see that, Dad?" I think he has to work out what it is that has enthralled me, realizing that the scale of a gust of wind in a 200' poplar was a lot more exciting to a three year old than the same wind in a scrawny bush in our garden at home, because the next time a gust starts developing its' roar, he comes and enjoys the spectacle by my side, maybe experiencing it through my eyes and ears as if for the first time.

Nature moving and roaring had other showpieces on the common. This time my Dad would lift me out of my push-chair and sat me on a wall. The wall had a railing to hold onto with gaps through which my legs would dangle. From this viewpoint I could look down and see what I had heard, the weir. Dark and sinister it was, water rushing from some hidden outlet over a waterfall and then swirling and clattering loudly over stones and rocks in a black, brown and gold, flashing turbulent energetic force that so fascinated me. I could sit there watching and listening for quite a long time because it was always changing. Moving water, be it weirs, waterfalls, flowing rivers, waves on a beach, even rain, seems to hold my attention in some profound way. I cannot count the times I, and many others, have thrown pebbles into lakes and rivers just for the pleasure of watching the perfect rings ripple outwards from the plop of entry, magically growing bigger and shallower, until they disappear into the flatness of the whole again.

Metallic Wards

Normal to me was the constant fear that I could be whipped away from the safety of the stairs and the scullery where my family lived with me, by racing ringing-bell ambulance to the hell-hole of Kingston Hospital. This could happen any day of my life. My bones fractured with very little trauma - I didn't have to fall downstairs or be punched in the ribs - my own muscles snapping into automatic tension to catch a ball or stop a fall would be enough for that sickening sound, the sudden pain and loss of power that signalled another break. The medical profession pronounced that such fractures were 'spontaneous', but they were not. There was always a cause, albeit minor and probably not seen by any observer. I knew that not even my bones were malicious enough to injure me for spite alone.

I am lying in a large cot in a long room full of identical cots. Everything is made of metal. There are metal blinds on the tall windows which are drawn up and down several times a day, each time with a fearful clatter. The locker next to me is metal. The plates and mugs which are brought out at every meal time are all grey, hard, noisy metal. There are movable screens on screeching metal feet moved by nurses to hide children from sight whilst they do mysterious and nasty things to them; there are metal trolleys covered in metal needles and other instruments of torture.

I am distraught at finding myself abandoned in this cold, hard world and I catch hold of the bars on my cot and shake them whilst crying my fury, hoping perhaps that a kind, familiar face will appear to comfort me. Instead a large round woman, dressed in a dark blue uniform with all the Sister's paraphernalia looms over me with a red face contorted with anger. She bangs her fist on my metal locker. "Stop making that dreadful noise!" she yells. I am terrified. I go silent. Rattling my cot and screaming is clearly not a good idea. From then on it seems that when I am upset, it is safer to be quiet. A bad habit of a lifetime has its' seeds sown in that metallic ward.

People seem to like me better when I am smiling. Hospital is filled with people, doctors and nurses, who are keeping me alive in the absence of my Mum and Dad. It seems wise to make myself likeable to at least some of them. Some of the nurses respond to my charms with great warmth and kindness as they gently wash and powder me. I fall in love with quite a few of them, especially the one with the golden plait which encircles her head like a halo, and the one called 'Nurse Mardi' who plays games with me and makes me laugh.

The Hospital is run like a military establishment. Every morning, at the change over from night shift to day shift, I hear the marching feet advancing along the corridor, getting louder and louder until the platoon of uniformed nurses burst through the swing doors and stand to attention, lined up in the middle of the ward. There is an inspection by Matron. The crisp white aprons and the carefully folded and pinned caps, or bonnets, have to be perfect. Watches have to be hanging upside down and in working order. Hair off the collar and scissors in pockets. The atmosphere is of rigid discipline and order. There is a very strict hierarchy with grades of women replaced by grades of men as it gets higher. That is how it is.

These spells of visitation to the other world of hospital end as suddenly as they begin. A ward round, a quick inspection of an X-ray by the God Doctor and "She can go" means my parents are told to come and get me as soon as possible.

My Mum comes to take me home from the Hell Hole, but first she has to dress me. I am not yet able to sit up but want to put on my vest myself. I am not going to allow her to put it on for me. I cry and wriggle, tugging the vest out of her hands. But try as I might, I cannot put on my own vest whilst lying down. A bemused nurse is looking on, not knowing if to intervene. Why I should remember this little scenario with such clarity is still a mystery, but it feels like this kind of battle where I refused help to do something I couldn't do myself was another of the bad habits I was forming. But maybe I was just angry with Mum for leaving me there in the first place.

The ambulance is not available for return journeys. We don't have a car so I am taken home on the bus. The ordinary world of people and buses, pushchairs and tea at home is in such contrast to the drama of institutional life that it is difficult to understand. Where do I really live, at home or in the Children's ward? Who has the power to decide? To whom do I really belong?

The authoritarian power of the State seems much bigger than that of my family. It seems that the NHS owns me, because I am 'handicapped'. I am begrudgingly let out on licence to my parents, but is it permanent? Can I be recalled to their nightmare metal, militaristic world where it is not safe to cry? How should I best behave to avoid this possible outcome? I cannot ask these questions aloud, so these dark thoughts and fears settle deep beneath the surface, shaping the actions that I feel compelled to take as I grow up.

The Wooden Walking Cage

When I am about three or four, I am kept in hospital for longer than necessary because they want to see if they could help me to walk. In order to do this, they bring into the ward a completely circular wooden frame that resembles a cage of sticks, or rods, but skirt-shaped. At its base is a wooden hoop

Early resistance

to which has been screwed many metal castor feet which swivel uncontrollably like the first attempts at tea trolleys that hit the wall and several pieces of furniture before coming to rest on the fireside hearthrug in a pool of slopped tea. I am not very big so this contraption is also small and light – so light in fact that it can tip over very easily.

The malevolent physiotherapist who thinks all this is a good idea, lifts me into the centre of her wonderful modern invention, makes me support some of my weight by clutching the top ring of wood – and then lets me go! She, and the other conspirators with her, make all sorts of weird noises they think will encourage me to walk along, pushing this crate from inside. I am terrified. It doesn't go in any controlled direction but wherever it wants, but only on the rare occasions it's too-many wheels are facing in the same direction. I know too that if I lean on it too much it might just go right over with me inside like a trapped hamster, all my bones broken. I cry every time the contraption appears until they give up, and I get sent home, my view of Stupid Adults reinforced once more.

CHAPTER THREE

The Fire Station

KINGSTON HOSPITAL AND WALKS to Barnes Common soon become a thing of the past. When I am four my Dad is promoted from 'Leading Fireman Mason' to 'Sub-Officer Mason' and we are sent to a new Fire Station in Sanderstead, South Croydon. Being almost a rural setting with a comparatively low call-out rate, Sub-Officer status was enough to be in charge of this post. We pack up, leave my Nanny's house and set off on a 45-minute journey for a new life.

What will this new life hold for me?

First Night in Another Land

I was dragged away from my window on the world that first night in our new house to start the routine so loved by parents in those days. I shared a big bedroom with my sister, but because she was nearly three years older than me, she was allowed to stay up later which meant of course that I was taken upstairs to bed on my own. It was still light. Children in those days were sent to bed after tea, at six in the evening, tired or not.

I lay in what might still have been a cot with sides, a precaution felt necessary to stop me falling out of bed and breaking bones. Everything is big and unfamiliar. A different smell, slightly musty, seems to seep out of the walls and outside birds are still chirping, dogs barking and there are new sounds of neighbours bustling about in their gardens.

As the evening gradually darkens I grow fascinated by the wallpaper all around me. It is covered in pictures which I remember as figures in big skirts or dark suits dancing across our bedroom walls. But oh dear! As I keep watching in the fading light those figures start to move all by themselves and the walls come alive! I don't like it. My heart starts pounding and tears begin to fall from my eyes. I call in panic to the abyss below me in which I hoped my parents still exist and would hear my wails. With great relief I hear footsteps running up the staircase. "What is it ?!" my Mum asks with the expectation that such loud calls for help must have meant a falling wardrobe or a giant spider. "The wallpaper!" I cry. "The wallpaper?" She was stunned into silence, not for the first time by the strange things which came out of my mouth. She does however switch on the light and suddenly the figures stop dancing remaining instead fixed in their repetitive patterns perfectly still. I am reassured, and eventually fall asleep.

For a while.

The night does not last as long as those in Mortlake. As the sun slowly rises in the sky a twitter, them some tweets gradually build up a sound I have never heard before. All sorts of bird song trill and chirrup getting so loud I almost have to put my hands over my ears. The dawn chorus! It almost seems to me the tiny little bodies must be sitting on my window sill with megaphones in their beaks because the volume defies the smallness of the source. I don't understand that when you live near a 3-mile wood as we now did, it is the sheer numbers of singers which create the capacity to fill the air with sound. Luckily, I find this less frightening than the dancing wallpaper, feeling sad when the light grows stronger and the marvellous chorus stop their concert. I am not sure I realize that in Spring this happens every dawn because I soon learn to sleep through it.

Sanderstead Fire Station

When we lived in Mortlake and my Dad went off to work, as far as I was concerned he had disappeared, only to reappear the next day from nowhere. When we move to our new house in Sanderstead it is different. My Dad can walk to work – and back again - in a minute or two. In fact, he can 'pop over' to check on things at home as often as he likes. He can also carry me across to the Station to show me where the big red engines live, the pole the men slide down from where they might be sleeping upstairs to reach the engines in a hurry, and the teleprinter which noisily clacks out the instructions of where to rush to next. He is not allowed to take me right inside though. That is against the rules.

The new house is not just an ordinary house. For one thing it is set in a cluster of houses all around the Fire Station Yard. The entrance to the yard is walled with four wrought iron gates, two small ones on each far end, and two big ones in the middle of the wall which open to let the fire engines in to be cleaned, stocked and for the fireman's regular drills.

The frightening but exciting thing about living so close to the Station is that we can hear the bells. These suddenly went 'down' very loudly, at any time of the day or night, clanging it's summons to all the men on duty to drop whatever they are doing, run, or, if upstairs, to slide down the pole to get downstairs in seconds, to clamber on board the Engines in a well-rehearsed and lightening quick operation. These machines are waiting behind the huge wooden doors which clatter open dramatically, allowing the red shiny vehicles to roar off to deal with the emergency. Often it is my Dad behind the wheel.

Between the startling sound of the bells, and driving off, the men have to wait for the teleprinter to let them know where to go, what has happened and if any other fire engines are coming too. My Dad tells us often that waking up at night to this sound means that within just a few minutes they have to get off their beds, become fully alert, assess the situation they might find and plan how to deal with it. They then have to race along in the dark in a large vehicle to an address they may not know and possibly find themselves in charge of a dangerous situation, a road accident or even a death. He tells us that this is what makes firemen die young, the suddenness, the stress of the call out, especially at night. I come to think he is a sort of hero, but am afraid for him all the time, now I can see what he is being asked to do.

The Tardis Outside

In Mortlake we lived upstairs, cutting me off from watching street life, but now I have a great view of the world by sitting on our front room window sill and looking out. I am fascinated by one of the wonders of our new settlement. It is a blue box, about 10' tall with a light on the top. The light flashes to call the attention of the local police force riding their motorbikes who pull off the road, dismount from their bikes and go inside the box with their policeman keys to answer the phone inside. Via this phone they would get directed by their Headquarters to zoom off to some urgent incident like a knight rushing to the rescue of some distressed damsel. I am very excited to realize I can watch this little drama happening through our front room window every day. My Dad, always disparaging of the police, says they are just being told their tea was ready back at the 'Mess', but I prefer my version of life-saving heroism. Later, when Dr Who chooses one of these magic boxes as his Tardis, I am not at all surprised that it is so much bigger on the inside than on the outside.

The Daily Routine

My days are very ordered by my parents, both of whom like routine. I wake early and wait to hear my Mum, the first up every day, come into our bedroom to collect me. I like to go down with her to watch her cook breakfast for everyone. I like the smell of frying bacon and watching her spoon hot oil over the fried eggs so that the yellow yolks developed a cover. I like baked beans but not really eggs, whilst my sister was the complete opposite. To be 'fair' my Mum cooks the same two breakfasts every day, alternating eggs and beans to try and keep everyone happy. My Dad just likes food. There is no guesswork about what we are going to eat each day. Roast Chicken on a Sunday, leftover chicken on a Monday, Stew on Tuesday, spaghetti on Wednesday, perhaps it was sausages or chops on other days, and always fish on Fridays because we are Catholics who don't eat meat because it would be a sin on that day.

My sister comes home from school and when my Dad is not on his watch at the Fire station, he comes home from his (moonlighting) jobs at midday, dinnertime, when we all sit round the table in the kitchen to eat a hot meal together whether I like it or not. 'Lunch' then was not a word. Everyone, except me, then dispersed to do their important work whilst I was sent off again to 'play'.

I hate it when my Dad goes out again and often hang on to his feet as he walks across the hallway to the front door, dragging me across the floor and shaking me off on the door mat. He is not allowed to take me with him to the fire Station, but he has other jobs, gardening and decorating to make ends meet. On a few very rare occasions he takes me with him to work, but to my disappointment I find I am left sitting on some stony wall whilst he digs and sows, or is otherwise busy and not paying me any attention at all. At least I have my own toys at home so begrudgingly I give up this particular fight and return to my more familiar rage that I am not going to school with my sister.

My Mum makes herself a cup of tea every day at 4pm. If she feels thirsty at 3.30pm she will say "I am thirsty, I wonder if it is time for my cup of tea yet?" glancing at the clock. "Oh no, half an hour to go" until the clock hands give her permission to put on the kettle. Next follows Mrs Dale's Diary and Children's Hour on the radio at five o' clock whilst we eat our tea. Tea is various things on toast, like mashed sardines, followed by cakes eaten at around 6 o' clock before being packed off to bed.

The same clockwatching which applies to her cup of tea also applies to my Mum's piece of fruit carefully peeled or chopped every evening at 9pm. "Is it nine yet?" This routine maps our week for years.

The thing which adds spice (literally) to this endless repeated programme of shopping, cooking and meal times is that my Mum eats different food to us. Whilst preparing our chops and beans she makes herself curry and rice. Mauritian food, hot and spicy with sometimes raw chilis on a side plate to chew alongside the hot food. She even eats this meal in a Mauritian way, piling the rice on one side of the plate and the meat-in-sauce on another then drawing a little of both piles into a 'mixing' space on the plate where she forked the two together until it was just right before putting it in her mouth. This procedure takes much longer than the rapid gobbling the rest of us do, made even slower by her insistence that the fork should be put down on the table between each mouthful whilst it was chewed properly. She is always the last to finish her meal, but makes us wait until she had done so before serving us any pudding. We respect this. There had been very little food around for my Mum growing up in Mauritius. She was one of ten children and the family was poor. Making the most of what you got made good sense.

My Mum misses the food in Mauritius, especially the tropical fruits such as guavas and pawpaw. Her misty-eyed descriptions made them sound so different and magical that I long to be able to buy her some. One time when it is her birthday I persuade my Dad to take me on a search for a real Mango which somehow, despite its' rarity at the time, we find on a market stall and I buy it with my pocket money. I wrap it up for her and she does indeed seem delighted to taste it again, which makes me happy.

The Battle of Food

Food is such a big thing when you are a child. I am not very keen on the stuff. There are only a few things I am happy to eat or drink. The first is something the new, kind, Government gives us free because, after the War, we now have a Welfare State which tries to nourish poorer children whose parents might not be able to afford fresh fruit. Whilst still in Mortlake my Mum pushes me in my pushchair on a weekly basis to some sort of council-run depot where we are given our Vitamin C ration in bottles of municipal orange juice and this completely delicious stuff call Rosehip Syrup. It is all dark pink and sweet and I cannot wait to get home to have some. We also seem to be obliged by The State to have a spoonful of malt every day which is like Ovaltine in syrup form and I like it as long as there is no added cod-liver oil which is disgusting.

Baked beans I can happily eat every day and I don't understand why my Mum won't let me. However, she relents when I am in hospital refusing to eat the horrible dinners they try to force on me. I feel clearly the hungry delight at visiting time when my Mum beams as she brings out the lovely, cold, baked bean sandwiches I had been longing for all day. I happily munch my way through a small stack, to the stern disapproval of the nurses. Apart from these sandwiches very distressing memories still haunt me from this era. Having my nose held whilst being force-fed. Being told to eat from a plate on which I had vomited (deliberately, they said); being plucked from my bed and put into an isolation ward for refusing to eat spinach. Later on, I remember defiantly tipping bowls of lumpy porridge out of a window by my bed. I hope the rats had a feast.

The only other food I consider a treat is milky, cheesy mashed potato, spread out across my favourite Lucy Atwell plate. I mechanically swallow little teaspoons of the stuff, motivated not only by the pleasing taste and texture, but also by the fun of slowly revealing the rosy-cheeked faces painted on the ceramic plate beneath. Unfortunately, most other meals are a tedious battle for my Mum to try and get down my throat. Many a half-eaten dinner is served up again for tea, reheated in a frying pan using dripping which changes the taste into something I like a lot more and eventually eat.

Keeping Warm

Our one coal fire, polluting though it is, is our main means of staying warm, especially in the winter. There is a lot of daily work involved in keeping this fire burning. Every day my Mum has to clean out the grate, scooping up the ash from the day before and binning it, whilst my Dad chops wood with an axe outside every morning to get today's fire going. Whilst I sit on the sofa watching, he screws up pieces of torn newspaper, pokes them into the fire grate amongst the chopped wood, and covers them with a light layer of coal (or coke) scraped out with special tongs from the coal scuttle, before setting them alight with spills or long matches. He then 'draws' the fire which requires him to place a whole sheet of newspaper over the opening in the hearth. Doing this creates a vacuum which, as the fire catches hold, sucks in the newspaper. Eventually the flames behind the paper grow bright and start to roar. More often than not, the sheet of newspaper itself then catches fire, the air escapes, the roar dies down and the smouldering newspaper falls into shards, hopefully in the fire, or the surrounding hearth.

The problem is that he is rarely still in the room to see this terrifying drama, having nipped out to do something else whilst he could, leaving me stranded on the sofa all alone to pray that the burning newspaper doesn't fall on the carpet by mistake, setting the whole house on fire and me with it. We do have a fireguard but he usually puts it in place after the event. Why?

This fire is not enough to keep the whole house warm. The other rooms which need to be heated are the kitchen, and the bathroom. We have paraffin lamps to try, often fairly unsuccessfully, to make these rooms comfortable to work, eat or bathe in. Paraffin is something liquid you have to get from a petrol station in a can. You then pour it into the tank belonging to the lamp, twist up a wick and set fire to it. It then burns for a few hours until all the paraffin has gone.

Upstairs is not heated, except the bathroom when we are having a bath. In the winter this means being so cold in bed that you can see your own breath and the net curtains being stuck to the inside of the windows with frost. To read in bed means we have to wear gloves. The only patch of warm is created by a hot-water-bottle, filled by a near (but not quite) boiling kettle and left in the bed whilst you get undressed. To make matters worse, warm air rising from downstairs condenses on the cold walls upstairs, making them damp, or even run with water.

All this was blamed for my chronic bronchitis which kept me sitting up at night in order to breathe, but later it turned out to be as much caused by the dust in the many wool blankets we layered on our beds to try and keep warm.

CHAPTER FOUR

Another Horrible Hospital

FROM THE AGE OF four onwards Croydon General Hospital becomes the place to which I am dispatched whenever my parents decide I need more help than they can give me at home following a fracture.

The smallest, sudden movement of tensing muscle can result in a horrible snapping sound. An unexpected twist whilst performing an act I have done safely many a time can do it. Coughing or sneezing can do it. Being picked up without warning; the car suddenly braking; slipping on the floor; catching a ball, even turning over in bed can do it. Every morning I wake up without any certainty where I will be by bed-time – still at home or in hospital?

Not all my fractures are major – cracked ribs or small bones I sometimes don't even tell anyone about. I just adjust my activities and movements to avoid moving the affected part as much as possible until it heals. Luckily children's bones do heal rapidly, at least to the point where the pain subsides – days rather than weeks. However, this is not so true of the more substantial fractures in arms or – worst of all – femurs. A femur fracture almost always means ambulances, X-rays, plaster casts or traction and weeks flat on my back in bed. Our local ambulance drivers call me the 'Fragile Doll' and know where to come for me without being given the address.

Children's wards in the 1950s are grim. Visiting time is only half-an-hour a day and children under 12 are banned for fear of their germs. For some perverse reason, the all-powerful adults in charge decide that even this paltry ration of parental love and comfort is not allowed the day before, or the day after, an operation. The justification is that we just get 'upset' when we see our parents, (cry with relief) so for me, the times when I am most in need of the warmth and security of my Mum and Dad, are the times I am most isolated.

I cannot even draw warm blankets around myself for comfort as I am always covered by a too-large metal cradle which is designed to keep the heavy coverings off my broken leg and the traction. It also blocks my view of the rest of the ward, but not the noises I hate – the metal trolleys, the wheeled screens and the crying children.

We children are not given medication to dampen pain. They argue we are too small and could easily be given an overdose. My only escape is sleep. I somehow put myself into a self-induced coma during which half-conscious times the conjured-up figure of Jesus, smiling kindly by my bedside, all-knowing and deep in my soul, is the way I survive the isolation.

After a few days of this, I am sitting up in my bed. The cradle has been removed as my fractured femur had begun to heal, no longer requiring the weight of the blankets to be lifted from my legs. Now there is nothing restricting my view of the rest of the Children's Ward.

The room is long with a separate four-bedded room at the end where the older children were given a little privacy. I am not 'older' yet. I am set in the middle of a row of cots and beds backed up against a wall. The floor is dark wood which is waxed and polished every day with a huge machine with giant circulating dusters pushed sullenly by a strong looking woman in an overall. I like the smell of the wax and watching the lovely sheen appear as she slowly works her way up the ward, moving all the beds and lockers as she goes. She likes me watching her work and smiles at me often.

Opposite our beds is a long wall of doors and windows. Through this glass construction a whole vista of Croydon can be seen. We were up one or two floors, looking down on roofs, roads, busses and people all tiny and far away.

Open Air Sleeping

The glass doors opened onto a balcony where, to my amazement and delight, we were sometimes pushed in our beds to benefit from the fresh air. Here on the balcony our beds were closer together so playing with each other became much more possible. Indeed, crawling into each other's beds became possible, if not really allowed.

In the event of rain, a green tarpaulin roof can be pulled out like giant canopy, making us feel like we are camping in tents. The strange hospital silence is replaced by the reassuring sounds of the real world - cars, birds, machines, people, reminding us that we are still part of something familiar and safe. Living insects fly onto our food. Real life has not ended. The little girl in the bed next to me is playing with a sewing set, using a big needle and brightly coloured wools. I ask to have a go and she lets me. I am happy, I have a friend and crawl into her bed to get closer.

Unwilling Witness

Being a witness to the way other children are mistreated causes me as much distress as my own. "Just slip out of the door when he is not looking" the nurse advises the young mother who had come to deliver her toddler-aged child to the ward. "Don't say goodbye because he will only get upset, and so will you". The mother does not look convinced but nevertheless takes the advice. "I will just go and get you a drink of orange juice" she lies to her little boy, as she picks up her coat and bag, turns her back and disappears through the swing doors without a backward glance.

The little boy is standing inside his cot, clutching the top rail over which he can just see. His face is white with fear. He is wearing pyjamas in the daytime, something all us children know to be an ominous sign of bad thigs to come. He stares at the closed door straining to hear his mother's footsteps returning with the promised drink. The door stays closed. The minutes tick away. The little boy grips harder on the rail, refusing to let go or sit down despite the onslaught of nurses who had their list of things to be done to him. "My Mummy is coming back" he said over and over again until his voice cracked and the tears came as he realised he had been tricked.

"You stupid, stupid people!" I think, watching this act of betrayal unfold. Adults protecting themselves from the pain they inflict on their children by walking out the door with their fingers in their ears. I feel very angry, but say nothing.

Encasing Carol

Carol Scott is three years old or thereabouts. She is on the bed next to me where she asks to be put because she knows me. I am her friend from the last time I had been a patient on the ward. In between times I had gone home and lived a comparatively normal life. She hadn't. She is a few years younger than me, a baby in my mind, but I am happy to be the chosen one as I feel concern for her.

Carol has been born with dislocated hips, a condition which is not that uncommon. The treatment is to wait until the child is just walking at which point they take the child into hospital and encase them from the chest downwards in a heavy 'frog' plaster. It has this name because the legs were forced wide apart and the lower half bent outwards and backwards, like a frog. A plaster bar is built between the knees and a cut-out square around the child's bottom so they can wee and poo. The idea was that in positioning the ball of the hip joint securely into the too-shallow socket, and holding it in this position for two years the bones would grow around this ball, correcting the deformity. The encased child has to be set upon a wooden frame in bed for the said two years whilst the bones grew.

The plaster is very heavy, but not so heavy a fairly strong nurse couldn't lift Carol out of her cot and walk around the ward with her a bit. The bar between the knees can be used almost as a handle at these times. Carol is a sweet and cheerful child, only really getting upset when the huge plaster cast has to be cut open and replaced with a bigger one as she grows. I am quite sure she thinks she lives in the children's ward with the nurses as her surrogate mothers. Her real Mum comes to visit sometimes, but Carol seems to barely recognise her.

Torturing Dawn

Carol was already plastered up when I met her. The full barbarity of the treatment handed out to children in the 1950's unfortunate enough to be diagnosed with dislocated hips does not make itself clear to me until the day Dawn arrives on the ward.

The swing doors swung open and I look up from playing with my doll to see a small dark - haired child walk into the ward. Her hand is held by a nurse but this doesn't stop her from swaying from side to side as she was led to a little chair by the huge windows over-looking Croydon Town. She was silent and unsmiling, her eyes big and round and full of apprehension. She looked all around the ward and our eyes locked. I kept the gaze for as long as I could, but became distracted by the contraption that was now being wheeled

Memories of Dawn

through the doors and over to, not a cot as her age might have suggested, but a bed. Dawn's bed. It was massive. It looked like a wooden four-poster frame slightly bigger than the bed itself, of the kind more suited to a strange hotel in a horror film, only missing the musty grey nets with trailing cobwebs. The most sinister part of the frame was at the bottom end. A wooden bar with notches evenly spaced along its length was attached horizontally to the two end posts, topping a railed fence which formed a large foot to the bed. There were ropes - what were they for?

Dawn is on her own. No loving parents are cuddling her, explaining what is happening, or reassuring her in anyway. This is all left to the young nurse who had been assigned to get her ready. Ready for what? The nurse is in no hurry to get her job done. She takes a long time to coax the little girl to take off her pretty dress, her knitted cardigan, her socks and shoes and finally her vest and knickers. Dawn makes no protest as she is dressed in a nightie although it was the middle of the day and the sun was shining outside. The nurse then, unusually, picks up the frightened little girl and begins to rock her in her arms. She walks about the ward over to the windows and then over to some of the children to say hallo. Dawn says nothing. I am mesmerised. I can feel a strange foreboding that seems connected to this silent child, the reluctant nurse and the medieval contraption surrounding her bed.

Matron bustles in and barks at the reluctant nurse to hurry up and get on with it. She is bringing more paraphernalia, little callipers of the sort I recognise. They were normally used to stabilize leg fractures through the technique of traction, as this has already been used on me. But Dawn does not have leg fractures. She can walk.

Finally, the nurse carries Dawn over to the bed whilst Matron drags over the squeaking wheeled screens from their storage space by the door, unfolds the sections to surround the bed, and takes Dawn and her nurse out of my sight behind her wall of mystery.

It is quite some time before the adults reappear and the screens are refolded and squeaked back into their place. I am almost afraid to look at what they might have done, but my imagination does not stretch to what they actually did. Dawn is still alive, yes. She is now lying in her bed flat on her back. Her legs have been encased in the callipers and the attached ropes which extend beyond her tiny pink bare feet are stretched tight then threaded through the middle two notches of the bar of the contraption.

The idea I gradually learn was to change the position of these ropes every day or two, placing them one to the next left notch, one to the next right notch, gradually forcing Dawn's legs apart like a star-fish in preparation for the main event - the frog plaster. Dawn's eyes search for mine and again we lock into an intense gaze. She is several beds away from me but her look burns into my memory, my heart and soul like no other look I have experienced. Terror, abandonment, reproach, desperation shoot across like a laser beam. She is silent. I am silent. But I am watching everything, recording everything. Dawn, like Carol, will not get up or walk again, will not experience family life, will not feel loved or safe again for over two years. The reluctant nurse knows this, but do any of them have any idea of the life-long harm they are really causing? Adults, I decide, are not only stupid, but cruel.

Tie-Down Nighties

Not all the children who arrive on the ward are as compliant as Dawn. Some put up a big fight when they realize they have been left by their parents in this strange and frightening world. They scream and break free from the clutches of the uniformed people, running about the huge room looking for a way out. For some, the way out is through those big glass windows upon which they throw themselves in desperation. Maybe their Mummy and Daddy were out there far down below getting on the bus home, having accidentally left them behind? Maybe they would hear them shouting behind the wall of glass and come back for them? I know they won't and guess what would happen next. On a nod from the Ward Sister the child's nurse vanishes, only to reappear holding a white cotton nightie designed for naughty children. It had two long cotton straps sewn into the side seams. Although the child is struggling the nurse undresses him, or her, carries them over to their assigned cot. With the usual loud metallic clatter, the side of the cot is lowered and the small over-powered person lain inside on their backs. The straps are then tied, or fastened in some way to the base of the mattress before the side of the cot is raised again, noisily locking into place. The screaming child is now pinned, caged, and left until they admit defeat and go quiet.

I watch all this in silence and horror. There are no cameras to record this. No family witnesses. The restraining nighties are always removed before visiting time and the child's own bedclothes put on. The Mummies and Daddies have no idea what has happened, or that this was normal, everyday practice. We child witnesses know we must not tell them.

Visiting Time

Tea is over at last. Not long to wait now. We have had our own clothes put on, our hair brushed, our beds tidied. A nurse goes over to the tall stack of red metal chairs which can fit on top of each other in enormous numbers. One at a time or two chairs are hauled off the chair mountain and deposited at the side of each bed or cot, including mine. It is empty now but won't be for long. The best time of the day has come, the moment when the past life of home and family, warmth and colour, kisses and hugs can return to our sides for a brief half hour. We all listen for the footsteps and the familiar voices. Who will it be today? Will they bring me something nice?

My Dad would often walk in by himself carrying his bicycle clips, having pedalled all the way from Sanderstead to Croydon. Sometimes at weekends my Mum and sister come too, but the rules of the Ward mean my sister, having not reached the magic age of twelve, has to stay out in the corridor with her germs, just peeping through the door. I wave to her, feeling sad.

I am hoping that in my Mum's bag are the things my hungry tummy has been waiting for all day. Not sweets, but my favourite delicious baked bean sandwiches! My Mum has not let me down. She takes out the package, unwraps the four little squares of white, (bread) yellow, (butter) and red, (cold mashed baked beans) and hands them to me. Both parents watch with indulgent smiles on their faces as I gobble them up. The passing nurses do not approve. They tell my Mum that she is spoiling me and this is the reason I won't eat my hospital dinners. My hospital dinners are full of greens and carrots, and even spinach, all of which make me feel sick. My Mum knows that I was just as 'fussy' at home, but she never lets on.

Sometimes I wait for my empty chair to be filled and no-one comes. Other children are surrounded by the people they wanted to see but my bed is surrounded by emptiness. The visiting time is not the usual half hour it seems, but much, much longer. I am full of disappointment, but I have already had a lifetime of practicing waiting. I switch myself into another gear, starting the clock ticking its' countdown until tomorrow's visiting time when someone will surely come, maybe bringing double baked bean sandwiches to make up for it. My Daddy is a fireman and has to go to work sometimes I know. Without a car and another child who was banned from the ward, it is also difficult for my Mum to get here. But when the nurse comes to retrieve my unused red chair to return it to its' stack, she knows I am close to tears.

If there is a good thing about my particular condition, it is that it always gets better, and I know it will. Each break mends itself, and the frequency of the breaks reduces. I only have to sit it out and I will be returned to our house and the familiar food, toys, and people as if it has never happened. No one talks about what it has been like, including me.

CHAPTER FIVE

The World of 141

141 LIMPSFIELD ROAD IS where I live my whole life. I do not go to Nursery School, friends' houses to play, or to stay with Nanny, Aunties or cousins. I do not even go outside to play with my sister and her friends until I learn to ride a tricycle and escape through the back gate, against orders, to pedal around the fire station yard towards the sound of young people having fun, hoping they will let me join in, which they did sometimes.

It is a very small world. I am told I need to be protected from 'cruel' children who may laugh at me or knock me about although nothing I have so far experienced of the nature of children who had the chance to get to know me, such as when I was in hospital, bore this out. I was usually sought after as a playmate because I had so many ideas of how to get up to mischief. I feel that somehow this is a justified punishment for coming out 'wrong', being an 'invalid'.

I learn to make the best of it, although in my imagination I had fantasies of just crawling out of the front door, down the pavement and into the living world of' normal life' before my Mum could hunt me down, snatch me up and tell me off for making holes in my dungarees by crawling on concrete. But even inside this restricted land, I can learn a great deal.

Life in The Garden

I always prefer being outside to inside even when it is raining. Our front garden which I see mainly from our sitting room windowsill, is my grown mainly to impress the neighbours and passers-by. It is very formal with neatly cut geometric borders and an immaculate lawn in the middle. My Dad grows roses and chrysanthemums in this garden which everyone admires. Already there when we move in there is a lilac tree which almost reaches my bedroom window. In the spring, when the tree flowers, I can open my window and breathe in the most wonderful perfume. I can barely remember ever going into this front garden and playing in it is definitely not allowed. The back garden however is completely different.

It is a sunken garden, below the level of the Fire Station Yard which gives it a secret feeling. From our back door there are four steep concrete steps down to the main level and all along the left-hand side of the garden there are two terraces of flower beds, dropping down from the fence which borders the yard with very unusual flint stone walls forming their edges, holding in the earth. There are also two rockeries flanking the steps, again forming tiered slopes from the house level to the garden level. In the top terrace there is an old apple tree which bears fruit. In the middle of the lawn is a cherry tree which doesn't.

There are already many plants in this garden including some which have grown through the cracks in the flint walls forming little puffs of colour and leaves in the Summer. However, both my parents like gardening and they spend hours planting and watering, deadheading and pruning this beautiful space and I love to be in it. My Dad builds a concrete path wide enough for my red peddle-along car which allows me to go up and down, although not turn around. I have to peddle backwards.

I learn the names of many of the plants and enjoy the magic of the seed-heads which can be gathered and sown for the following year. But even more than this I enjoy the birds which are varied and plentiful, because they keep me company. I learn to sit very still so as to not startle them. When I do this they come closer and closer, especially the sparrows which bounce around the ground just a foot or two away from me. Very occasionally rare birds appear, including lovely turtle doves with wing feathers which look like they have been bordered with orange paint.

I want to learn more about the birds and animals, trees and plants but there is nowhere to go to do this, apart from books which are not really written for young children. I feel strangely part of this natural world and do not like being dragged in by my Mum when it rains, or the wind starts blowing. Strangely I am not even afraid of thunder and lightening when I am outside in it, despite being very afraid of both things when I am indoors.

Smog

Even home isn't always safe. One day when I am playing indoors because it is winter, I look up at the front room window and, to my horror, everything outside it has disappeared! Our front garden, the shops and houses across the road, all gone. Instead there is a thick yellowish blanket of nothing. I am really afraid and scuttle under the table to hide my head in a cushion. No one can comfort me. "It is just smog" doesn't mean anything to me. I am still a bit young for one of my Dad's lengthy explanations of smoke and water vapour. I just want everything to go back to normal. To my relief the blanket gradually turns to smoke, then mist, then the houses and shops start to reappear along with the cars, headlights blazing, creeping slowly along the road. Sometimes someone is walking in front of the cars with a torch to lead the driver safely forward.

Most of us have coal fires burning in or front rooms to keep warm, and to heat the water for a bath. Many of the 'Shouts' for my Dad as a Firemen are to put out fires in people's chimneys caused by sparks igniting soot from these coal fires. All of us pay people with long funny brooms to come and sweep out the build-up of soot in our chimneys in case this happens to us. Everywhere in London, and all the big cities, have walls blackened by the smoke from these coal fires. Smoke and fog together make smog, and smog really is something of which to be afraid. People die from breathing it in.

One day, when I am about six, in the newspaper it says the Government are going to stop this. There is something called 'The Clean Air Act' which means we have to stop burning coal in our fires and burn something called 'coke' instead. Apparently, this does not make as much smoke and the air stays cleaner. My parents both think this a great thing.

Gradually my Dad has to go to less chimney fires. The Government also organise for the whole of our cities to be cleaned up. Although it takes years, London, the blackened city I know, is scrubbed, revealing beautiful yellow stonework and gold highlights, the most dramatic example being the Houses of Parliament themselves with it's magnificent 'Big Ben' sparkling in the sunlight.

Kings Wood

The abundance of birds in our garden is partly because we live very near the Kings wood, which is one of my favourite places on earth. I am told it is three miles long, stretching all the way from Sanderstead to Warlingham, behind the houses, away from the roads, left untouched for ever.

Unlike everywhere else, things in the woods just get left to do what they do naturally – bomb craters from the War are not filled in, fallen trees stay where they fall (unless they block a path) and are allowed to gradually break down. Best of all thousands of bluebells are allowed to flourish every spring forming a blue carpet as far as I can see, filling the air with a perfume which you just cannot buy in a bottle. My Dad warns us that we must not pick the flowers as they are there for everyone. We might even go to prison if we do.

Sometimes my sister can be persuaded to take me with her friends to walk in these woods, and sometimes we go as a whole family to have a picnic in the dappled sunlight, the birdsong and the green ferns. It seems like another world.

The Birth of the Garden Shed

I am sitting on the windowsill, via the top of a chest of drawers, in our bedroom upstairs. From there I watch interesting things going on in our back garden. On this occasion it seems my Dad has commandeered the help of my sister, aged about seven or eight. Right at the bottom of the garden they are standing in a cleared space on a concrete slab my Dad has created himself with bags of cement and wooden planks. It has dried and is ready for the next stage of the project. I can only just hear their voices as my Dad hammers away at large pieces of wood set out on the ground with a lot of heaving and squealing from my sister who looks very tiny to be doing what she is being instructed to do. But then, to my amazement, on the call of "Now!" my Dad and his little helpmate push up a huge frame, bigger than them, with four corner posts and joining struts all of which fall into place making an empty box upon its' concrete floor. When they both stand back it remains upright all by itself. I am so impressed I clap! I had witnessed the birth of our garden shed! Over the next few days I watch as the sides are created from overlapping timber slats, nailed from the bottom to the top in quick succession, window frames put in, then windows, a roof, and finally a door at one end. The wooden slats are painted with some dark stuff to prevent them rotting and the door and windows painted green.

Much more banging and sawing then goes on inside, from which we are all banned until it is finished, but one day, my Dad finally carries me down the path he had also made himself, opens the green door, and sets me down upon the bench to admire his creation from inside. It was another world. A musty smell like no other of wood and oil and sawdust. Tools are hanging on pegs except for the all-important vice attached to the bench. There are shelves full of tins and jars, holding screws, nails, nuts and washers all of which I love to sort and count, feeling the hard metal and the soft sawdust. All is suffused with the pleasant smell of machine oil used to clean and preserve the various blades and hinges.

Under the bench is stuffed a huge hoard of old bits and pieces which will "Come in useful one day". As my Dad makes and mends everything in our house I love to spot the 'recycling' of door handles, bits of cupboards, pieces of lino, picture frames, springs and scraps of leather reappearing in a new form in some of his creations, which of course proves his point.

This little separate domain of my Dad is where he does not mind if I get a bit dirty, or risk splinters, where he always finds a job for me, and where I watch as he creates new things from raw materials with the tools I love. He lets me try them all - the wood plane which shaves slivers of wood from rough surfaces until they are smooth; the rasp which can be used to soften sharp edges; the little hack-saw I can manage, unlike the big saw that was too heavy; the chisels and hammers used specially to make wonderful dovetail joints that would never come apart; the spirit-level and the mitre block for making perfect picture frames.

By watching this shed, and all that was in it, appear at the bottom of our garden - once only a flat patch of weeds and brambles - I learn that we have the ability to imagine something and then to make it *real* with the power of our minds, the skill of our own hands and a bit of help when we need it.

CHAPTER SIX

Prison Education

"COUNT BACKWARDS FROM A hundred" demands the lady with the clip-board.

"Ninety nine, ninety eight, ninety seven..."

"Oh dear, you are as bright as a button, aren't you?"

I didn't answer again. Her words are saying one thing, her face another. Being told you are as bright as a button, is usually experienced as a compliment, something good of which to be proud, but her expression, tone and voice says something very different. My evident intelligence is a problem both to them and to me. 'They' are representatives of the Local Education Authority who are charged with the legal requirement of providing me with an education. I am causing them great difficulties because they have nothing to offer which seems appropriate. There is a Special School in Croydon to which I could have been sent, but on their own admission, I would not really receive an education there. They could provide speech therapy which I clearly didn't need as keeping me quiet was a bigger issue than helping me to talk, and physiotherapy which was also not useful to children with OI (Osteogenesis Imperfecta). They are slightly unnerved by the realisation that I could count and knew my alphabet before I was five and genuinely concerned that I would be bored quickly by the very basic developmental curriculum then taught in all special schools. The obvious alternative was just to go to the local mainstream primary school with my sister, but it seems this was never even considered.

I cannot walk and my bones keep breaking for very little reason. There are no safe wheelchairs available for disabled children, only large push-chairs which, as the name suggests, require pushing. Crawling round the floor in school as I do at home is out of the question. There are no extra staff in schools to physically assist children, especially to manage the toilet, and anyway, there is no way any Head Teacher is going to take on the responsibility of a child who is more like a china doll than a proper kid. The authorities do not know what to do with me.

The sad, almost tearful expression which is aimed at my button self was evidence of what they think is an even bigger problem than their lack of a suitable school. They believe that being 'handicapped' is tragic and that my life is therefore going to be small and miserable. My ability to be aware of this is not something to celebrate. How much better it would be for me if I was 'Off with the fairies' as they assume most disabled people are, happy to weave baskets in our high-walled institutions, oblivious of what we are missing.

Although very young, I know there is something wrong in this 'What a shame you are clever' attitude and I don't like it. I have no sense at all that my whole future is doomed, given that tea-time seems a long way off and next week a life-time away. As usual I look to my parents to see how they are reacting to this strange lady and her clip-board. I had answered her questions right but was still made to feel I had done something wrong. I was clearly not being what I was expected to be. My Mum looks irritated, but I am not sure with whom - me or the lady? My Dad looks as delighted with me as always. I am somewhat reassured. He speaks to the lady in a tone which redirects the problem back at her. The only offer made is Home Tuition for five hours a week. It is accepted by my parents without a fight. I have no idea what they are talking about.

Mrs Ness

The door-bell rings at 10am sharp. I have already been put in place on the sofa in our front room. A small table is standing in front of me with paper and pencil case. I am dressed and combed and know somehow that I have to behave. The room is very quiet. No other children to share my lonely lessons, only the ticking of the clock, and, in winter, the crackling of the coal fire in the hearth. My Dad is at work, my sister at school, my Mum busy in the kitchen. Mrs Ness comes bustling in. A large round woman with a smiling face, she speaks to me cheerily with a Scottish accent, but I struggle to listen. I do not want to be there. Her main goal is to teach me to read and to do simple sums. Out of her bag she produces boring 'Janet and John' books which I have to look at, reading aloud to her until she is finally satisfied that I can read well enough that more interesting books could be introduced, much to my relief.

Books, Books and More Books

I quickly become an independent reader. Books open up a whole new world of stories, ideas, and people who come to keep me company through the wonderful combination of the writer's skill, and my imagination. My Dad joins us to the local Library and takes me there almost weekly, carrying me around from shelf to shelf as I choose my next stack of books.

The speed of my reading grows as does the size of the books. Hans Christian Anderson, The Brothers Grimm, The Arabian Nights filled my head with fantasies, far-off lands and creatures with three heads whilst Enid Blyton took me soaring away to the Magic Faraway Tree where Dame Wash-a-lot threw her dirty water down over the heads of the poor unsuspecting Saucepan Man and little Pixie. My heart beats in excitement as the inhabitants of that marvellous tree raced to get back to its top-most branches so they could climb down to the familiarity of their home before the strange, magical land they had been exploring moved off forever, with, or without them. Would they make it in time?

Arthur Ransome delights me with a whole series of children's adventures in a boat I recall, under the title of Swallows and Amazons. Even more to my hungered imagination are the two girls, Tamzin and Rissa who owned horses, Silver and Cascade and lived in Martello Towers, possibly on a beach in Hastings. I love the idea of a round house with windows looking in all directions.

It hadn't passed me by that all the children in my books were able-bodied so Heidi, by Johanna Spyri, and The Secret Garden, by Frances Hodgson Burnett hold a special place in my heart. In both are children who could not walk and are befriended by 'normal' children who seemed to like them. I read these two books over and over again. "You are not reading Heidi again, are you?" as I asked for it for the seventh time. In the total absence of characters who reflected my reality, these two fictional 'invalids' were the nearest thing.

There was a problem though. Basking in the radiant attention of their non-disabled saviours, the two children, a boy and a girl, in two completely different circumstances, start to get better. Their little frail bodies start to get stronger and fatter as they eat their cheese and breath the nice fresh air until, lo and behold, they get up and walk! As Peter kicks Heidi's wheelchair away down the mountainside because she no longer needs it, it is apparent that both these child heroes of mine have only been 'handicapped' by their own minds, by fear and self-pity, by over-protection and lack of courage. There isn't really anything wrong with them at all. They stand up and became 'normal'. That is the happy ending! Am I just imagining that I cannot walk?

This view of disabled children seems to be the only one around. My Dad arrives home from somewhere with bags full of second-hand comics for my sister and I. As well as

'The Beano', 'The Bash Street Kids, Denis the Menace, Mini the Minx and other such unforgettable fun, there are piles of 'Bunty and Judy' magazines full of stories about rich girls at boarding school, learning ballet and riding horses.

'The Courage of Crippled Clara' tells the story of a young girl trapped in her wheelchair living a lonely miserable life until her demise is noticed by the kind-hearted heroine of the story who manages to heave the poor thing onto her horse where she was suddenly high up and able to move around on four legs. This does not lead to a great insight into the need for disabled children to have friends and something interesting to do, but to the endless hope that if we stop behaving like disabled people, we will improve, get better, be less of a problem to the people around us. It is our fault we are disabled.

I however, am pretty sure that if I had a horse I would fall off and break all my bones, and this would not lead to the Great Recovery with rejoicing in the street. But I do not have any defences against the darker message implicit in these stories. If I don't get better, my life will be miserable and that misery will be somehow to do with me not trying hard enough, not making enough effort.

CHAPTER SEVEN

Filling the Empty Hours

FIVE HOURS A WEEK 'education' leaves a lot of empty hours to fill. Like many young children, I wake up early, listening for the sound of life from my parents' bedroom next door. My Dad and my sister are the busy ones, the lucky ones with a life outside the house. My Mum feeds and brushes everyone, then the two busy ones leave to join the world and we are marooned in a quiet, empty house with nothing much to say to each other. If it was a Mrs Ness Day, I have to get washed and dressed, books and pens found, and to be sitting nicely in my place on the sofa before the door knocks at 10 am.

If it is an 'empty' day, my Mum shoos me outside to play in the garden, and starts on her list of chores. We have no television, only a big 'wireless' which is on all day. She listens to 'Workers' Playtime', a programme aimed at factory workers in their break times, and 'Listen with Mother' which I do, although she doesn't, more often using this sit-down time to have a little nap.

Washing Day

Washing day, Monday, is a day of hard labour. Firstly, the boiler has to be dragged out from its corner, filled with cold water and lit underneath. The water takes a long time to reach boiling point which is necessary to remove the stains and dirt from the cotton sheets and work-clothes which most people use. Mountains of laundry are then fed into this machine, stirred and removed with heavy wooden tongs. They are rinsed in cold water in the sink, each article needing a lot of strength to wring by hand. My Dad would try to come over from his Watch (shift) at the Fire Station to help wring, especially the sheets. We do eventually get a mangle at some point, but even this is hard work. I want to try. I want to be the mangle person. But it is too hard for me, except squishing the water out of handkerchiefs. Not a great help really.

Starching clothes is something my Mum does. I am not sure why. One day I think she overdid it. She and my Dad go outside to get the clothes off the washing line where they hang to dry. They are all very stiff. My Dad comes into the kitchen and stands them up all over the floor, shirts and skirts, nighties and pyjamas, frozen in their hanging positions, arms upraised like an invisible army surrendering to the Mason family. I think it is the funniest thing ever.

Toys

For children, toys are really important. Without playmates or other distractions, they are even more so for me. I love to play with the spinning top with the push-down handle; the dolls' pram with the folding canopy and 'false' bottom; the wind-up goose which clacked its wonderful way all down our hall; clockwork trains with its own railway lines; jig-saw puzzles and construction kits. We have a huge box of something called Bayko. I love this set of fiddly and quite sophisticated elements which, under the right management - mine - can become realistic houses with bay windows, doors, steps, windows which opened, beautiful roofs and chimneys, each one different to the one before, limited only by my imagination.

In fact, fiddly and me go together very nicely. Usually thought to be a 'boys toy' the little screws and nuts of Meccano are no obstacle to me as I construct extraordinary gadgets and machines with pulleys and wheels. One favourite is a hanging box-like cable car, one end of which I persuade my dad to fix to the curtain rail in the front room. I can wind little objects in the box right across the room and up into the air, although my Mum soon makes him take it down again.

Even more fiddly is a set of tiny objects which could be collected in packets called 'My Miniature Garden'. I am absolutely fascinated by this. You have tiny little brown plastic flower beds, studded with little holes. In the same packet come tiny, tiny plastic flowers and separate stalks and leaves. Each has to be detached from a plastic framework, painstakingly put together with each individual flower which might only be 2mm square – you almost need tweezers to handle them, but not me – pushed onto a stalk and then leaves attached. The magic bit, which I think is what really captures my devotion, was that then, because of such clever design, each plant can be placed over a hole in your flower bed, and then, with a specially designed tool also supplied, planted into the hole where it suddenly stands up, a perfect, brightly coloured miniature 3D plant – I love it.

I save my pocket money to expand my flower beds into a whole garden with trees, paths, lawns, little ponds, fences and crazy paving. My sister and I have a big dolls house and this tiny plastic out-doors gradually surrounds it, making it very difficult for anyone except me to play with, being an extremely controlling head gardener as I am. Luckily my sister is happier playing outside, jumping off things.

Christmas present toys are extra special because our parents have to save up lots of money to buy them. They ask us what we want and then we have the anticipation of, maybe, getting it. This Christmas eve I have finally managed to fall asleep after hearing, I am sure, the sound of the reindeers landing on our roof. 'Father Christmas' has left at least one present on the end of our beds for the morning. So excited am I that I wake up when it is still dark and can make out the lump by my foot, just asking to be opened. I fight off the temptation to act on my impatience, as I know it is too dark to really be morning and I might get into trouble, but in the end, I just can't wait.

As quietly as possible I slowly peel off the paper and discover, to my joy, a toy sewing machine which really works! Now, being a clever sort of kid, I realize that although it is dark, this little battery-operated machine has its own light, and when I push the button and switch it on, I can just about see well enough to try it out on the conveniently supplied piece of cloth. The problem is that this little machine is surprisingly noisy so, as it happily clacks away on its maiden voyage of chain stitch. My bedroom door is flung open to reveal not one, but two angry adults asking me what on earth I thought I was doing at only four in the morning!

There are some toys we love but which become illegal. Cap guns for example. You can go into a shop and buy little tins containing coils of blue paper impregnated all along with little dots of gun-powder. When placed correctly in the cap-gun and the trigger pulled it made quite a substantial bang with associated flash and rather satisfying smell. Even better than guns I thought were cap-bombs. These are heavy little metal torpedo-shaped toys with a blunt nose which was sprung in some way. You put one of your gun powder 'dots' in the nose of this little contraption and then go upstairs from where you open a window and drop it from a great height into the path of an unsuspecting adult. I think this happily reminds me of dropping things on my Nanny's head when we lived with her. When it hits the ground the cap goes off, making the person targeted by our mischief jump out of their skin, and us double up with give-away laughter. I think our parents ban these before the law does, spoil sports one and all.

As a disabled child, water pistols are a great therapeutic aid - the more powerful the better. I can just sit there and threaten and squirt, making my sister in particular really furious as I drench her in cold water every time she tries to

Patrolling the doorstep

get past me. As I often patrol the back door by sitting on the doorstep and she is too young to have a front door key, this allows me a lot of revengeful power requiring very little effort. Unfortunately, it also works the other way round with me being literally a sitting target for her to soak back, so it is a mixed blessing overall.

Dick Townley's

'Dick Townley's' is my favourite place in the whole world. Set in the middle of a parade of shops in Sanderstead it brims with things I want. It is a toy shop - an emporium of wonderful things from fishing nets (to catch tadpoles in the pond up the road), to clattering windmills and colourful kites which come alive when the wind blows. There is an electric train set in the window which, when I drop a penny in the slot outside, will magically start to chug around its tracked journey past tiny trees, under a bridge, out of sight behind a miniature mountain, and then re-appear round the bend to complete its' journey in front of my delighted eyes.

There are two collections of things which are of special interest to me, for which I save my pocket-money each week. The first are little packaged jokes. These included floating 'sugar-cubes' made of foam; red-faced soap which, as the name implies, smear some red coloured substance on the skin you are supposed to be cleaning, and bits of metal which, when dropped on the floor, sound like a plate smashing. I can't wait to get home with my latest purchase in order to trick anyone I can with these very funny treasures. The smashing plate joke is one of the best and most enduring sources of irritation to the adults around me because, even though they have been caught out by the ominous sound several times, each time they are dropped everyone automatically cringes and runs to see what has happened, only to find me giggling amid my scattered metallic fun.

Another great success of this joke collection is a set of plastic spiders which, as the picture on the package suggests, you can use to frighten people who are frightened of spiders, such as our Auntie Therese. This particular deception requires the help of my very willing and able sister. When our Auntie comes to stay one Christmas, we put these spiders in her bed. We wait with barely suppressed excitement to see her scream as she lifts open the bedcovers and finds the eight flat black identical spiders on her glistening white sheets. Luckily, my Auntie quickly realises the nature of the game and hops about squealing with 'horror' as she battered the poor spiders with one of her stilletto-heeled shoes, making my sister and I laugh so much my Mum comes upstairs to find out what all the noise was about.

The Wireless Set

I fail to hide my latest injury from my parents. Although I try to explain that I am sitting very still and don't want to be carried anywhere because I am practising being a statue, they are not fooled. I have been left in bed upstairs in the bedroom

I share with my sister but she is out at school. I have only the wireless set for company. This is a large, heavy wooden affair, plugged in at the end of my bed but placed right next to me on the counterpane so I can fiddle with the knobs myself. These knobs are not easy to click or turn, but I spend a lot of time tuning in into different channels, some of which bring strange languages and news from all around the world, like magic to my bed.

As the day gradually passes the room becomes darker and the sun starts to set outside. I call down for someone to come and switch on the light but no one hears me. The light in the wireless set appears to get brighter as the room dims until it is the only source of brightness or sound. I love listening for my favourite songs, 'Tubby the Tuba' and 'The Little Red Monkey'. Best of all was Children's Hour' every tea-time at 5'o clock. Just for me the people in the wireless read stories and play funny things which make me laugh.

When I am mended and can go downstairs again, the wireless set comes down with me and is returned to its' normal place where we can all hear it. Workers Playtime is enjoyed, but all my family like funny programmes best. My Dad loves the 'Goons' and my Mum likes 'The Glum Family'. I liked 'Jimmy Clithero', a character with an odd sounding voice playing the part of a child who keeps outsmarting the adults around him. Ha! ha! Good for him. We all love Gerard Hoffnung recounting the 'Bricklayer's Lament' with his barrel of bricks going up and down, a story which is requested frequently by listeners. Everyone in my house stops what we are doing to listen yet again to the ridiculous story. It makes us laugh every time.

Sunday dinner is served up to the haunting theme tune of 'Desert Island Discs', a piece of music forever conjuring up the delicious smell of roast chicken and Yorkshire puddings.

On Sunday mornings there is also a special programme of messages and musical requests for British Forces Posted Overseas. My Uncle George is a Major in the British Army. His wife, my Auntie Marcel and my two cousins Billy and Fifi are living overseas in Germany in Army accommodation. I imagine them glued to their wireless sets like we are, waiting for a message from home.

The Television Set

A wireless is good, but it is only sound. Today a new box of magic is coming into our house which has a little screen with actual moving pictures to watch, as well as the sound of people's voices. I cannot wait! The knocker on our door bangs. Dad has come home from work at the Fire Station during the day to oversee the installation of this new marvel.

He answers the door and shows the two delivery men into our sitting room where I am bouncing up and down with excitement. The television set is unpacked and plugged in to check that it is working. To my delight the screen lights up and moving pictures appear. The set has four wooden legs which need to be screwed into the base of the set so the men put it on the floor upside down to carry this out. To their amusement I bend myself into a 'C' shape with my head also upside down so I can see the amazing black and white pictures of 'Muffin the Mule' whose strings are pulled by a lady with the poshest accent I have ever heard. The BBC has entered our house and changed my world.

At that time, around 1957, we become one of hundreds, maybe thousands of households where men are hanging out of windows. or precariously balanced on roof tops twisting and turning a huge metal contraption called an aerial, shouting "Is that it?", whilst standing in a doorway with their gaze on the screen of their TV set, was a woman or an older child shouting back up at him "Yes! No! That's it! No, gone again" as the little dots on the screen came together to form a perfect moving picture, only to break up again into a buzzing mass of flying dots. It had to be just right. My Dad tells me the aerial is picking up a signal from the Crystal Palace Transmitter and one day he will take me to see it because it is huge and very impressive.

Leather Gaitors

Misguided adults still cannot give up their attempts to make me better. When I am about seven, another attempt by the medical profession to get me on my feet are the leather gaitors they make for me. These are carefully made thick leather supports into which my legs are encased and fastened by a series of brown leather straps with buckles. The only problem with this design is that the leather cast includes my ankles and half my foot. A specially-made pair of boots were then laced on, over the whole lot. The result is that when I am placed inside these things and then stood up, I cannot move my ankles, and cannot therefore keep my balance. I am like a plastic walkie-talkie doll and I know immediately that, just like my dolls, I am going to end up flat on my face on the floor if anyone lets go of me for more than ten seconds. Even my sister who is quite keen on the idea of me walking in these things says "It's not going to work. She's going to fall over." Much to my relief a family decision is quickly made to put the gaitors, and their boots, up in the loft where they never again see the light of day.

I myself have no great desire to be able to walk. I think the people around me really believe that all I dream of is being just like them but I have no such dreams. The only 'me' I know is one who cannot walk, but who can do many other things, some of them very well. What I cannot understand is why they are not helping me do those things which I can. I cannot skip but I can turn the rope – why don't the Stupid Adults get this? It would be so much easier to send me to school to learn things from books which I am well able to read, instead of experimenting on my fragile body with crazy contraptions which are dangerous and doomed to failure. They are obsessed with this idea that to make me more 'normal' would make me 'more happy', but to me, 'normal' people seem weird, and definitely not very happy, so why would I want to be like them? I just want to be allowed to be myself.

SPB 391

Oblivious to my parents huffing and puffing as they have to quickly fold up my push chair whilst carrying me and several bags of shopping before an impatient driver pulls away, I like travelling on the bus. I like the bus conductor coming along with his little ticket machine hanging round his neck. He asks us where we want to get to and turns a handle to issue the correct little bit of punched chard in exchange for a few pennies of our money. Like many children I collect these tickets. He manages to do this in a swaying bus without falling over, which impresses me.

I like the names he calls out as we reach various stops, especially 'The Swan and Sugar Loaf' which is the name of a pub at which point the road forks and we have to go left, up Sanderstead Hill and through the cutting to reach our home. Some of the busses are Trolley busses with long arms growing from their roofs in pairs to reach parallel wires which electrify the motors somehow. I even like riding in the bus in the dark and rain, seeing my own face reflected in the window through the slanting drops. I like watching the passengers get on and off, all different.

This is ending though. Today we are getting our own car. We all wait outside our front door, just inside the yard, for this long- awaited treasure to arrive. "Its Green", says my

Dad. “No, it is grey” argues my Mum. “Everyone can see it is blue” states my sister. For once I think they are all right. It is one of those colours which changes with the light.

It is an Austin A40, registration number SPB 391. My Dad has bought it on the ‘Never Never’ against his usual habit of saving up and buying things outright. For the next three years, because of this huge expense, there is little we can ask him to buy which doesn’t get the answer “Not until the car is paid for”.

We pile in and all go for a short ride, giggling and squirming with excitement, Mum in the front, we children in the back. The car changes our lives because we can now go out on picnics, country drives, to visit my cousins, and to see my Nanny back in Mortlake. Best of all, we can go on holiday every year to the seaside. I just love hanging out the window and feeling the wind blow my hair and face, especially as its’ smell changes to the salty beckoning of sand castles and fish and chips.

Sometimes, on a long journey home, it is dark and raining with the strangely comforting sound of wipers rhythmically swishing the windscreen so my Dad can see where he is going, and we don’t have to worry about anything at all except feeling tired and dozing off in the gently moving car.

CHAPTER EIGHT

My Inner Artist Rises Up

The Cracking of the Slate

MY SISTER AND I come back from our holidays in Wales with a slate each. It is in a wooden frame with a slate pen. I can draw pictures on my slate and then wipe them away with a damp cloth or sponge, and do another one, and then another one. I love it. I can draw ladies in big skirts with feet sticking out from each side of the bottom and hands with fat fingers. I can make patterns in their dresses which look pretty. I can make them smile then wipe off their smile with my cloth and make them cry instead. I can make their hair long and straight or short and curly. I can put big bows in their hair or sometimes hats. My sister is busy drawing on her slate too. She comes over to show me what she has done. Oh dear! my sister is nearly three years older than me, therefore maybe ten years old and her drawings don't look like mine. I can tell straight away that they are much better than mine in ways I could not possibly do myself. I feel a great wave of anger and frustration. I don't like my drawings anymore, or my slate, which I pick up and bang on my poor sister's unsuspecting head. The slate cracks and we are both crying. My Mum comes to see what is wrong but is as usual baffled by the scene before her. Our slates are taken away as if they were the cause of the trouble and my sister and me are both furious. Who would have thought drawing could cause such drama?

Stolen Paper

My Dad comes home from the Fire Station every now and again with a big pad of paper for each of us which he had 'released' from their stationery cupboard. We both like drawing and there never seemed to be enough paper, so these big blocks seem sumptuous to us. I had seen my sister do 'good' drawings so practise hard to be able to do the same. I spend more and more time each day with a pad, pencil and rubbers making the pictures of people, trees, animals, houses, flowers I have in my head become visible on the paper before me.

My Mum sewing

The adults around me soon start to tell me that I am good, talented, clever but this praise means little to me. I am driven by something inside me which wants to control the movements of my hands so that the images on the paper more and more reflect the images in my mind. To me, they never do so I would have to try again. I am pleased with the feeling of getting better, more skilled, but it can always be improved upon. There is always an element of dissatisfaction which drives me on. When I ditch the colouring books with their pre-ordained outlines and pick up the grey sugar paper, blocks of watercolours and lovely soft paintbrushes in order to paint my own pictures, my interest becomes a fascination.

I am usually sitting on the floor with the paper propped up on any piece of furniture available. I have the blocks or tins of water colours spread around me and a big jar of water with brushes standing in it. My Dad keeps telling me to take them out when I am not using them to stop them from permanently curling as they are pressed out of shape by the sides of the jar, but I keep forgetting. How do you paint a pond of water so it looks wet? How do you paint a tree so it looks like it is blowing in the wind? How do you mix up colours to paint skin? These experiments completely absorb me. The clock is not ticking because time does not exist. The joy I feel when I achieve the effect I am after is deep. The delight I experience when something unexpectedly beautiful emerges makes me feel I am going in the right direction, directions which are written on an internal map that has nothing to do with anyone else's opinions, ideas or judgements. These are my happiest times.

As I keep working at it, my competence grows. I think about the books I read in which the illustrations are as important as the words. Some of them are stunning in their beauty - way beyond my skills - but others, especially the line drawings are often so different to the pictures the text has created in my imagination, that I think I will try and do something 'better'. I badger someone to get me some drawing pens with the deadly black ink that cannot be washed out if you spill it on anything. My Mum warns me about this several times a day but I am careful now.

I love drawing highly detailed pictures that take hours to complete. "I don't know how you have got the patience" is commonly said as people look somewhat longingly at my efforts, but they don't understand. It doesn't take patience. It is deeply satisfying to me, more like a meditation. Whilst I am doing it, my mind is elsewhere, in a timeless state, yet completely focussed on creating this unique work by the fine collaboration of my own brain, eyes and hand. 'Patience' I think, 'Is what I need when listening to you lot'.

I need better paper than the stolen Fire Service pads which were off-white and too absorbent for the ink drawings I am doing every day. Paper seems to be an expensive thing, especially the beautiful white smooth stuff called cartridge paper, which comes in drawing pads of the sort I only get given for my birthday. Typing paper was the next best thing. It came in packs with many, many sheets. My Dad buys me one of these packs and puts it in a cupboard in our 'dining room'. Every day I go into this room, open the store cupboard and take out my daily ration of two or three pristine sheets. I bring them into our living room where I get lost in my latest efforts.

To make them last longer I often draw on both sides even though the first drawing may show through into the second. Painting paper is also rationed as are the water colours I diligently use until they are no more than a soggy trace of colour around an empty cell in the paint tin. I dream of going into an Art shop with a wad of money to buy anything I want which I can then use without any restraint at all. I could just try out any idea I had. I could practice using materials I had never even seen before. I could do messy stuff without getting told off. Heaven!

CHAPTER NINE

Becoming a Bride of Jesus

IT IS FRIDAY AND that is always fish and chip day because we are Catholic. If I was to eat meat on a Friday, this would be a sin and I would not go to Heaven when I died. Instead I would go to Purgatory, which is a particular horror only we Catholics are brought up to fear. Purgatory is some cold dark land between Heaven and Hell where you can suffer for long enough to fully repent for your wrongdoings while you were alive. If you have endured enough pain and misery, and said "Sorry God" enough, you might be forgiven and allowed through the Pearly Gates after all. I am not going to risk it though so I am happy to eat my fish. My Mum usually served it with peas which were the only green vegetables I like so Friday is a happy dinner day.

I cannot remember how I first learned about Jesus or who it was who told me that he loved all children, including me. I was convinced that He was always watching over me in a loving sort of way, listening to my prayers and anything else I cared to say to Him. Someone, possibly even my Mum, said that Jesus had made me disabled for a reason. He had some kind of job He wanted me to do and I could only do it by being different to everyone else. I know this is the truth because I had worked it out myself anyway.

In fact, I know, though I keep quiet about it, that I chose to be born disabled for that very reason. I know that one day everyone will see the purpose of it all. I refuse to be a victim of the circumstances of my own life. When I am alone in pain, in a hospital bed, the fully technicoloured image of the kind Jesus hovering over me, seeing what my parents were not allowed to see, makes it bearable. Oddly, going to church on Sundays seems to have nothing to do with this experience of kindness and big ideas.

What is this thing called 'sin' How do you become a good person? If Jesus knows everything I am thinking then He will know that my intentions are always good even if I am sometimes a bit naughty. I am told in my catechism lessons that children can only commit 'venial' sins, for which we can do penance and get forgiven, but adults can commit 'mortal' sins which are much worse, like killing someone, and once you had done that you went to Hell where you were burned forever, however sorry you are. It seems like it is best to avoid that fate by not committing these sorts of sins. This is easy because they are all listed in the Ten Commandments which God had sent to earth on a tablet of stone which didn't wear out like my Mum's paper shopping lists which ended up in our rubbish bin.

They all made good sense to me, especially the first three. "Thou shalt not kill; Thou shalt not steal; Thou shalt not tell lies." The commandment not to kill includes killing disabled babies like me before we are born. I discover this soon after

I discover adults have abortions, an idea which fills me with horror. We Catholics don't do it because God says all human life is 'sacred' - more valuable than anything else. My Mum and Dad did not know that I had OI before I was born, but it makes me feel happy to know that even if they did, I would probably still have been given the go-ahead.

First Communion

Now I am eight I am old enough to become a 'Bride of Jesus' which happens at a special event called our First Communion. Before our First Communion though, we have to take our First Confession in order to clean up our souls so that they are in a fit state to receive the Body of Christ in its bread form.

There is a very rigid ritual involved in this act which I have to learn without making mistakes. I have to go to church on a special 'confession' day with my Mum. Inside a few sad looking people are sitting, or kneeling at various places in mostly empty pews. Some are clutching chains of beads (rosaries) and muttering prayers to themselves. Others are lighting candles and placing them in frames of candle holders before making the sign of the cross, gathering up their shopping bags and escaping back out into the sunlight. It is very quiet, like a library. I do not feel I can talk above a whisper, but I do not know why. I don't remember reading any bible stories which said Jesus didn't like noise, but I don't feel I can argue my case.

We take our place in a queue outside a small cupboard like construction, which has a door. People take their turn to go in and come out of the door and I am next. I think I know what is going to happen because we have been given scripts and made to practice in our catechism lessons. I am very nervous though. Will I forget my lines? Will the sins I have remembered be the right sort of sins? Should I make up some better ones, or would Jesus know and decide that was a new sin in itself? Would I fall off the seat inside and break something? Would Father Ward guess who I was when my Mum had to lift me in although he wasn't meant to know who it was who had committed such terrible things? I look anxiously at the face of the last person leaving the box. Does she look forgiven?

Finally, the door is open, waiting for me. My Mum lifts me out of my chair and carefully places me on a waiting bench. Inside, I can now see, the cupboard is partitioned by a dividing wall into which is set a 12" square grille, and behind that is lurking Father Ward. It is dark and musty and there may be spiders. I feel quite keen to get out again. "Forgive me Father, for I have sinned" I squeak, as I have been taught. "How long is it since your last confession?" "This is my first confession" the script continues. "Have you killed anyone?" Father asks me. "No!" I answer in shock. "Have you been a robber?" "No!" "Have you been telling lies to your Mum and Dad?" "No!" "Well, what have you done then? "I suddenly can't remember the list of naughtiness I have carefully prepared, and start to giggle. "I don't always say my prayers at night like I am supposed to" I say, with false contrition.

"Ah, well, go and say five 'Hail Mary's' for your penance, and you will be forgiven" says the voice behind the grille, followed by "Shall I get your Mum?"

Becoming a Bride of Jesus means I get to dress up in a little white Wedding Dress, complete with veil, to take part in a sort of ceremony with a few other children. We have been prepared for this over several weeks, in the catholic version of Sunday School (catechism). I am allowed to go to this every Sunday after Mass, much to my amazement, although, unfortunately, it is very boring and hard to understand.

On the big day I am not allowed to eat breakfast because, for the first time I am going to swallow the body of Christ in the form of a little round wafer of bread which I mustn't chew. Christ apparently did not want to end up in my tummy full of half-digested beans, and who could blame him?

I take my place in the line of children taking their First Communion, afraid that I might forget to make the right responses to Father Ward in the manner and timing in which we had been drilled. I do it all right though. I open my mouth when prompted and have a tasteless little wafer popped in where it sort of melts, so I can swallow Jesus.

I am dressed in my bridal gown and given a basket full of rose petals to carry. At some point after the swallowing procedure we children have to throw the petals all about, although I have no idea why. This is the most fun bit, and the party after.

I do swallow Jesus, but nothing happens. It could have been mashed potato. Oh well, if he is everywhere and already knows what I am thinking, this eating of him seems a bit unnecessary anyway. I know already that adults are an untrustworthy bunch, but I am happy to be part of it all, even if it seems mostly nonsense.

Aline and Lawrence Mason

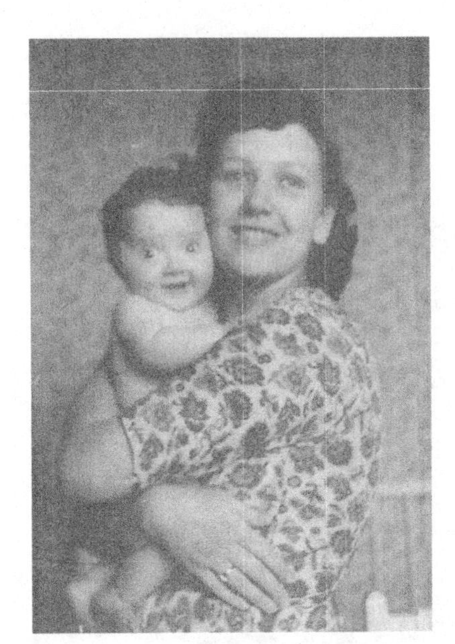

Home at last

My first car

My sister Brenda

The Daily Sketch photo of me and Pepe

At Art College

CHAPTER TEN

Silver Linings

THERE IS NO ENID Blyton 'Magic Faraway Tree' in our garden, but next-door new lands do appear when a new family moves in. Mr and Mrs Lily have moved away with their two daughters and the Andersons are taking their place. 'Next door' is within my reach, unlike the rest of the world. Our house is a semi-detached council house with front and back gardens. There is a path which leads from our back gate which opens from the Fire Station yard, passes by the back door-step where I sit, all the way along the back of the two houses, past next-doors door step, then around the corner of their house and all the way down to their front gate leading onto the main road. There is a small hinged gate dividing this path in two, but it opens. When it is open I can slide off my doorstep into the seat of my tricycle and pedal the whole length of this path from back gate to front gate, and back again. Will the new owners of the path let me do this? More importantly, would there be little Andersons who might like to play with me?

A shadow appears through the glass on our back door followed by a knock. My Dad opens the door to reveal not one but four people. A man in uniform just like my Dad's, a woman with red, fly-away hair, a bald baby with a big head and equally big blue eyes, and, to my joy, a little girl of about six. She has short thick straight blonde hair and a round face with pink rosy cheeks. She does not look shy although she doesn't get a chance to talk much on that first meeting. Her eyes are shiny with excitement. They look full of fun, and hopefully mischief. I like her straight away. I have learned to look very carefully at the faces of people who see me for the first time. I look for signs of shock, fear, awkwardness, all of which make me feel embarrassed and a bit shameful. I saw none of this in the faces of the Andersons. The Mother, Betty has a powerful personality. The rest of her family glance at her to get guidance on how to react to their new neighbours, one of whom seems a bit different. She seems to exude a message to her flock, without saying it, that difference is not something to fear, but to learn from. If her little girl, Lynne wants to be friends with me, then that would not be a problem. I am excited.

They chatter to my parents for a while, then continue down the path, opening and closing the hinged gate and disappearing indoors through their own back door, taking Lynne with them.

I go and sit quietly on my back-door step, watching for signs of this new life next door. Sure enough, after not too long their back door opens and the little round face pops out looking all around at her unfamiliar garden. I am still quiet but willing her with all my might to turn her head so she can see me waiting for her to come and play. I have chosen a toy I think she might like and am holding it in full view but pretending to play with myself. She does see me eventually, and the tempting toy, which she does not seem that excited about. She seems more interested in talking to me. She hangs on the gate, as we have that first chat, but does not yet have the confidence to open it and come through.

Suddenly everything has changed for me. This new land next door has opened up my world a little. Betty is happy for us to leave our little dividing gate open so I can pedal the whole length of the path even when they are out. This is a

Portrait of Evelynne 1961

new attitude from people outside our family, not the hostile one my Mum has taught me to expect. Lynne, who is three years younger than me has an equally warm and generous take on life. Soon she bounces out of her kitchen, flings open the gate to come and sit with me on my step.

My three-year-older status makes her happy to take my lead on the endless games of imagination I love to play with her, making up fantasy adventures which we enact in our own 'built' environments. When it rains or is just too cold, Lynne comes into my house to play. To the amazement of the adults, but not to me, Lynne automatically gets down to play on the floor, crawling around under the table where we make caves out of blankets, or dress up as nurses or teachers who torment our doll-children as adults have shown us to. Sometimes, if we are lucky, baked beans on toast are allowed to be eaten inside one of floor-level creations. Lynne only gets back on her feet when it is time to go home.

Lynne goes to school so I spend a lot of time waiting very impatiently for her to come back. Our time during the week was after school and before tea, usually about two hours of fun. At weekends things were less predictable as her family did things, or went out at different, irregular times. I am told I mustn't keep shouting for her to come out because I am rude and being a nuisance. I have a brain wave, and sing instead: "Love is like a vio-LYNNE!" I bellow it out with all the volume my puny lungs can muster. No-one appears, but I hear mothers in both houses laughing.

I hate it when Lynne is ill or away of course. My parents worry that I am too dependent on my one friend and need to stop being so demanding, but Betty makes a point of telling us that Lynne is just as disappointed as I am if we are unable to have our playtime together. She seems to understand that it matters to me to hear this. I am not used to adults who are sensitive like this. From this friendship, and the support it gives I am able to build a wall of resistance against the onslaught of negativity hurled at me by the prejudices of the time. I experience an uncomplicated connection with a 'normal' child who likes being with me, likes my games, and whose mother thinks this is a good thing for both of us.

It doesn't last forever, around three years, but it doesn't have to. By the time I am twelve, Lynne is still only nine and the age gap begins to cause difficulties. I am keen to press on with the business of becoming a delinquent teenager and Betty begins to get a bit concerned that I need friends more of my own age, which is true. Finally, they move from next door to a house of their own. I am sad, but know that a Lynne-shaped building block will stay with me forever.

Getting Pepe

Not having many friends to play with, I get the idea that a puppy would help fill the gap. This does seem a bit strange because I am actually quite frightened of dogs, especially big ones like Alsatians or Boxer dogs, barking and growling at me ominously on many a shopping trip.

My parents are unsympathetic. "Who would look after it?" and "Dogs are such a tie," were the repetitive responses to my pleas. My campaign continues unabated. Unfortunately, my next tactic, which is to keep singing: "Daddy wouldn't buy me a Bow-wow!" only seems to irritate him, especially after the first ten renditions. For those of you who are not of my generation, the words went like this:

Daddy wouldn't buy me a Bow-wow, Bow-wow
Daddy wouldn't buy me a Bow-wow, Bow-wow
I've got a pussy cat
And I'm very fond of that –
But I'd rather have a Bow-wow-wow!

You can see his point. "Oh well, I will just have to buy my own bow-wow," I think.

At nine years old with no earned income and about six pence a week pocket money, I realise I will have to sell stuff in order to get the money. To this end I write a heart-rending story about a little girl in a wheelchair with no friends who had a puppy. The puppy got run over. I illustrate this with lots of blood red crayon and make the whole thing into a little book held together with ribbon.

I have an uncle Peter who visits us regularly. On one visit he sees me busily tying up my book and asks me what I was doing. With him the whole sorry tale of my longing and my heartless and mean parents falls on more fertile ground, probably because he doesn't have to live with the outcome of my appeal. Without much explanation, he asks me if I would be willing to type the story with a proper typewriter which he could lend me. As using a proper grown-up typewriter seems like an exciting thing in itself, I of course say "Yes". He makes it clear that the purpose of all this is to remain a secret.

A few days later he brings the typewriter and I re-write the story. My parents are a bit mystified at what is going on, but my uncle's idea works a treat.

He sends my story with a covering letter to a newspaper called '*The Daily Sketch*'. Their heartstrings are sufficiently twanged that they offer to buy me a little puppy of my own. My poor parents have little choice but to agree, and in only a few days my uncle, a newspaper reporter, a photographer and a quivering basket arrive at our door. Some kind of interview then happens and photos are taken, but I am not paying much attention, being totally mesmerized

Pepe and me

by the basket and its contents. At last someone opens the lid and out springs a little apricot-covered bundle of fluff, which, being terrified, hurtles round the room then wees on the carpet. It is love at first sight.

My uncle's wife Maria is Italian. She suggests the name Pepe, which we all agree seems just right. The dog is a miniature poodle, at that time un-clipped resembling a tiny brown sheepdog with dark shiny eyes and nose. He is full of life and intelligence. Being able to understand everything I say to him, I am convinced he can read my mind.

Having accepted defeat in the face of my determination to get what I wanted, aided and abetted as I was by my uncle, the whole family becomes very attached to the little animal, laughing a lot at his funny antics which are many. He is indeed a companion during some of my most isolated years, although an accident with a bus ends this episode even faster than it began. There was something weirdly prophetic about my little storybook as it turned out.

One lasting benefit of this episode is that I get over my fear of dogs for ever.

The Rec

Some days, particularly during the school holidays I get lucky. Today is one of those days. My sister has learnt that "Can I take Mickey out for a walk?" got a much better response from my parents than "Can I go up the Rec and flirt with the boys?" which, now at the age of twelve or so, and rapidly developing into a young woman, is a very natural thing to want to be doing. I am still only nine, and I am more interested in the freedom I feel flying about on the swings. I am strapped into the pushchair I still had to use out of doors and find myself, to my delight, part of a small group of children walking up to Sanderstead Recreation Ground, without any adults supervising us.

There are two parts to the Rec, like two fields side by side. The first seems to be left a bit wild with long grass and wild flowers. The second is mown grass and much 'tamer'. In the distance, a long way back from the road but very visible is a little hut in which a man sits all day and every day, keeping an eye on things. We head for this hut because the man knows us. I guess he has told my sister he would keep an eye on me if she wanted. I have mixed feelings about this because he is kind and friendly and the inside of his hut reminds me of the haven of my Dad's shed. He has a kettle, makes himself tea and shares his biscuits with me. Outside his hut he has planted and tends a wonderful flower bed, brimming with colourful blooms complete with butterflies. This rainbow oasis can be seen blazing from the main road. However, I really hanker after being in the thick of the child world of play and fun, not sitting in the hut with an 'old' man being kept safe. I don't want 'safe'. I want adventure.

Riding the Jigger

Today my dream is coming true. We walk past the hut and turn left along a narrow dirt path towards a copse of trees. As we get nearer to the trees the objects of my desire appear, hidden from view from the road by the trees, a secret wonderland just for us. There were tall swings, not like the puny things you find in people's gardens, but big sturdy swings even teenagers could stand on and create a stir. I loved to sit on these swings because I went much higher, and swung for longer so the sensation of flying was intense and exciting, but still perfectly safe as long as I gripped the hard metal chains really tightly. I am by now heavy enough to work the swings up myself, albeit with a great deal of effort, so I can be left to amuse myself like this for quite a long time while my sister runs off with her friends.

However, the best, most exciting thing of all is a piece of playground equipment we call the 'Jigger'. Yes, we are going over to it! My sister asks one of her stronger companions to lift me on to it, which he does, quite gently I notice. The Jigger consists of a long wooden platform seat which is punctuated along its length by metal handles. I sit astride the wooden seat close to and clutching one of these handles. Other children get on behind me and in front of me. All look flushed with excitement. This particular plaything is different to all the others in that only works as a collaboration between several children of different ages, sizes and strength. We young ones would sit waiting for the 'ride' to begin whilst at least two older 'youths' (sometimes they doubled up into two pairs, making four) took their places standing up at each end of the seat, which was suspended from the huge frame on hinged metal struts. The older children, sometimes including my sister, would then start to lean backwards and forwards, holding onto the struts to use their strength and body weight to 'work up' the Jigger. The more energy they put into it the higher it goes. The seat upon which I am sitting starts to move backwards and forwards, rising and falling then rising again. We riders start to giggle and call for them to go higher. The workers, encouraged by our obvious enjoyment put more and more effort into their gymnastics until we, with pleats and skirts flying in the wind, are squealing with fear but not wanting it to stop, ever. I do not worry for one minute about falling off.

I do not remember anyone falling off, but the sad day did come eventually when the all-powerful adults who could not bear us having any sort of risky fun deemed this piece of equipment too dangerous.

Riding the jigger

They were dismantled and removed from playgrounds all over the country. Like cap guns and all the best toys and games, they were made illegal, kept alive only as good memories in our last generation to experience them.

The Walking Frame that Works

Having been stunned by the impracticability of all past attempts by various medical professionals to help me to be more mobile, my Dad decides to try and do something useful himself. Mr Bishop is a fellow fireman, who also has a daughter, Lorraine, with OI. He had made her a walking frame that could be steered by its' power-source child walker, and, most importantly, could not be tipped up however hard you tried. My Dad wanted to make me one and had got the support of Mr Bishop to do the welding.

One day his creation appeared in our dining room. We are all called in to see this object as he was rather pleased with it. It was a metal frame following three sides of a square wider at the bottom than the top. Each corner post ended with a rubber stopper of the sort you see on the end of elderly people's walking sticks. These were raised above the ground by the clever positioning of the wheels. There are two side wheels 'rescued' from an old push chair, and one big swivel wheel attached to a triangular extension on the front. The top had wooden, padded, leather covered arm-rests round three sides, leaving the back open for access. My Dad who understands me better than most, does not encourage me to get in and do a performance with everyone watching. He says "It's here when you are ready to try it", then wanders off to do something else.

It is a few days before I venture back into the room to study it properly when no one is around. I look at it from all angles, and push it around a bit with my hands. It is nothing like anything I have seen before. Eventually I find a way to stand inside it, taking most of my weight through my arms on the arm rests. That's all right. I feel safe enough. I take a step forwards and the frame moves with me, just a little bit. Yes, it is under my control! I take a few more steps and then try to turn it towards the door. It turns easily, Wow! I see an empty dining room chair. I walk towards it, then turn and back up so the chair is right behind me, then sit down on it. Yes! It is all safe. I practise getting up and down from the chair a few times then rumble over to the door. I use the frame to push the door wide open, then step out, upright, to find an audience to whom I can show off. Look everyone! My crawling days are over.

My Walking Machine

Using this frame is not about being able to walk

unaided, but about being able to go outside under my own steam. However, I notice when once upright, people start to treat me differently, even though I am so tiny. It seems that something clicks in their heads that I am not a young child or incapable of speech. I notice a small increase in the level of respect in which I am treated. More people address me directly rather than the people with me. Although one young child asks my Mum if I am real or a 'Dolly' most people seem to start to notice the difference. This is weird. But I am not keen to get back on the floor again.

One day I get my parents to lift the frame over our front door step and go off for a walk, all by myself for the first time. I walk past the Fire Station, past the houses with the big poplar trees, past our church and on towards the shops. I find a little wall to sit on for a rest and then turn around and come home again.

As the days progress so does the distance I can manage. I have never been given any physiotherapy or treatments of any kind to help strengthen my muscles and bones, but weightbearing and walking about do both. Thanks Dad.

CHAPTER ELEVEN

Not Growing Up

I DON'T SEEM TO be growing up. My sister, my cousins and all the children I know are getting taller and wider, gradually changing shape to more closely resemble the big adults around us who may not be a completely different species after all. I am still tiny, the height of an average four-year-old. My Dad takes me to the chemist in Warlingham and sits me on the weighing scales. "Two stone and ten pounds" he announces with a tone of slight wonder as if he couldn't quite believe that a ten-year-old child could weigh so little and still make so much noise. I am confused. Inside I am thinking and feeling as I know a ten-year-old should, but the outside isn't catching up. The outside is too little and still crawling around the floor like a toddler, not even toddling in fact. My Dad's quizzical expression as he compared me to a bag of groceries show me that I have got a big problem. He doesn't know what to do with me.

I had seen adults in wheelchairs on the streets dressed as giant children. They wore great big sandals and white ankle socks. The women had their hair pinned in ugly styles. I was horrified. This fate though was not one I ever thought would happen to me as they seemed much more 'different' than I was. But these fearful memories are beginning to take on a new meaning. I am aware that the clothes we wear change as we grow older. There is a thing called 'fashion' and everyone, especially girls, want to buy and wear the clothes that are in it, including me.

My problem is two-fold. Firstly, nothing fashionable fits me, especially shoes. Indeed, it is much easier to find brown leather children's sandals in sizes 10 and 11 than it is to find the kitten-heeled winkle-pickers for which I long. The second problem is that the deranged adults who buy my clothes seem to think that I should continue to wear baby clothes for the rest of my life. Now I realise with a sinking sense of foreboding that those poor 'handicapped' people I had seen on the streets had been dressed on purpose like that by the staff who looked after them in order to try and keep them child-like and easier to control. They hadn't been allowed to grow up.

Well they can lump that. I am going to take charge of how I look from top to toe, starting with my hair. I am no longer going to allow either parent to cut my fringe half-way up my forehead. I am going to let it grow until it gets in my eyes. I am going to peep out from behind this scary screen with a sultry expression and look good.

I am going to choose my own jumpers and cardigans, or persuade my Nan to knit me smaller versions of the 'Sloppy Joe's' she made for my sister. I am going to insist that the only shoes I will put on will have pointed toes even if the high heels I desire cannot be found in the shops. I will find blue jeans for little children and throw away the check cotton bibbed overalls my Mum made for me in endless succession all through my crawling years. I will wear black tops and blue jeans because the adults say I look like I am going to a funeral and it annoys them, as I intend it to.

I will plaster my face in Pan-stick, including my lips whilst highlighting my eyes and eyelashes with lots of dark liners and mascara until I look like a mini, ghost-like beatnik. Only by waging this war against the deranged adults can I show the world that I am 'normal' and therefore require a 'normal' life.

The Blinding Flash.

I am lying on the grass under our cherry tree. The day is warm. The sky is blue with slowly moving cotton wool clouds that change shape as I watch. The scent of cut grass is drifting into my senses. Out of the blue a terrible thought comes to me. Suddenly, as though a time release bomb has gone off in my brain, the small and limited picture of my life expands in a flash into a much bigger multi-coloured view of the past, present and future. I realise for the first time I am always going to be 'handicapped'. I am not going to become an able-bodied 'grown-up', ever. I am always going to be the same as I am now, only older.

I saw that the world into which I was inevitable heading was one big competition. A competition for boyfriends, love, work, money, everything, and I am not going to be able to win. I did not have what it took. I was too small, too physically weak, too strange, too poorly educated to hope to beat all the millions of competitors. I was stuffed!

There is no one to tell of this horrendous internal revelation. I believe that everyone else around me already knows this and were hoping to keep it from me for as long as possible. If I give voice to my fears, everyone will only confirm them to be well-founded. Indeed, my Mother has already warned me that "No one will ever love you except your own family". My entire family assume that I will live at home with them forever. Their biggest fear was what would happen to me when they died. Up until such a time I would be kept safe, eating baked bean sandwiches and listening to the wireless. If I could find things to do, even paid work at home to keep me occupied, that would be nice but not necessary as they would always look after me. This is the inevitable result they believe of my impairment and its' consequences.

I do not need to hear this. What I want to hear is that the future is not really set in stone, that I can make a place for myself because real human connection is always possible if I am given the opportunities I need to make them. I need to hear that I am loveable just the way I am. I need to hear that I can create meaningful work for myself using all the gifts, talents and insights which I have in abundance. But reassurance was something I have to live without if I stay confined in this house, with this tiny cast of characters, with their lack of imagination. **I have to get out.** On this momentous sunny summer afternoon, I shift myself into another gear. I start to work towards a future which only exists in my imagination, clutching any straw of hope from any unlikely source, fuelled by a terror of a future life full of nothing. I couldn't let it happen.

CHAPTER TWELVE

Mr Stone is Called to My Rescue

WHEN I AM TEN Mrs Ness has to retire for health reasons, causing the authorities a dilemma. My parents take me to an appointment with the director of education to see if he can offer something useful to me.

I am aware that I need to charm this man as he obviously is very important and has a lot of power over my future. I smile and gaze at him, finally presenting him with a drawing I have just done whilst the adults are talking about me. He seems duly charmed and pins the drawing up in his office.

It is unusual he tells us to need someone to teach a disabled child up to the same educational standards as a 'normal' child. The Local Authority, Surrey County Council (SCC), have no-one on their books who fits the bill, so the Director of Education makes a special request of a friend of his, a retiring head teacher, to take me on.

Mr Stone

A very quietly-spoken, elderly man wearing an immaculate suit with a bow tie walks into our living room. He introduces himself to my Mum, and then to me, with the same perfect manners and attitude of respect. I like him straight away.

Cyril J Stone is a dapper sort of gentleman. He is the one commandeered to be my home tutor. He was asked to teach me English, maths, history and geography, and to tutor me through the 11+. I still would much rather be at school, with other young people, but at least this man can listen to me. He listens to me wittering on about everything in my life, from my desire to paint my nails white to how excited I am by the Beatles. He always appears delighted by this stream of consciousness, never breathing a word of what he really thinks.

He is also a brilliant teacher for me, as he teaches by the oral method – asking me challenging questions and making me work out the answer. He teaches me critical thinking skills, and the beautiful logic of mathematics, all by debate. Written work was always done as homework. He teaches me algebra, another form of logical thinking, and I become good at it although I can never see what possible practical use it could ever have.

The best times, however, are the last fifteen minutes of each two-hour session when he sips the cup of coffee my Mum brings into him (at exactly the right time) and reads to me from classics such as *Oliver Twist* whilst I listen and draw pictures, inspired by what he is reading.

Portrait of Mr Stone

I have never been read to before and it seems extraordinary to me – almost magical. It is like two minds working as one, and not something many of us ever experience other than momentarily. Something quite profound happens in those precious minutes, but it is still beyond me to say what it is.

11+

Mr Stone brings in piles of past 11+ papers for me to practice filling in. The law says that all children are entitled to take this examination at the age of eleven, to sort out the bright from the dim and thus send the two different sorts of children to different sorts of schools where we would be prepared for different sorts of jobs and future lives. I am also entitled to take this exam although I cannot recall anyone talking about what implications there were for me if I passed or failed. My sister has not passed her exam and has been sent to Riddles Down Secondary Modern School, a two-mile walk away from our house which she does there and back, five days a week, and where I know I cannot follow.

For me, these papers are like filling in a puzzle book and I enjoy doing them.

When Mr Stone is here we do them aloud - "Which is the odd one out?"; "Which is the next in the series?"; "What is the right word to fill the blank in the sentence?" I was good at it, and it was fun. He leaves me some to do as 'homework' which I am happy to do.

On the day of the exam Mr Stone is not allowed to sit with me. The Education Authority sends a stranger - an 'invigilator' to sit with me so there can be no chance of being 'helped' by anyone. I have to do it myself. I find it quite exciting and am pleased as he tucks away my papers, sealed in special envelopes, to have a chance to see how well I do in comparison to all the other 'normal' children, who are also taking the same exam on the same day.

There is a long wait before we hear anything and I have almost forgotten about it, but one day, a special letter arrives. Inside I know are my Results. There are three of us, my Dad, my Mum and me at that early morning gathering. My Dad opens the envelope and reads it to himself while we watch his face. His face doesn't seem to know what to do. Surprise, pleasure and concern flash across it. He frowns and reads it again. Then he reads it aloud. "We would like to congratulate Miss Micheline Jill Mason on achieving a score of something % in her recent 11+ Examination, placing her in the top 10% of pupils in her cohort. This means she has been awarded a place at Whyteleafe County Grammar School for Girls starting in the Spring Term of 1962...."

"What?" I think. "Am I to go to school then?" "Am I really clever?" "Where is Whyteleafe?" My Mum looks shocked. I am not sure if this is good news or not, but it certainly isn't failure. Maybe things for me are going to change. Maybe I have shown them all that I am worth something, that I deserve a life!

The second letter arrived only a few days after the first. It is an apology. Not because I hadn't achieved the score or won the coveted place, but because they shouldn't have told me. As I was 'handicapped' and there was no support in mainstream schools for children who needed wheelchair access or physical assistance, I obviously could not take up the place. They were very sorry if we had been given the wrong impression. They would however take my abilities into account when working out the number of hours of home tuition to which I would now be entitled as a secondary age pupil. My Mum looked relieved, my Dad looked furious. I went a bit numb. Just how mad was this world in which I was living?

The Head Teacher at Whyteleafe County Grammar School had been party to the same bureaucratic bungle as us. It seems that some sense of injustice had been stirred in her bosom. She wondered if I could be a sort of non-attending pupil of her school, and if some of her girls would like to visit me at home to create a human link between us. She invites me to visit on one of their open days where she has some volunteers all lined up to look after me and keep me safe.

Whyteleafe County Grammar School is at the bottom of Mitchley Hill, a very steep drive down which we rarely go as it is not the way to Croydon or the shops.

The school itself looks to me like the sort of place which belongs to The National Trust, where you buy tickets to view and have tea and scones in the Tea House, like at Heaver Castle. Even once inside my impression does not change much. There is lots of dark polished wood and sweeping staircases. The dining room, where we do indeed have tea and cakes, has huge French doors which open out to a view of their sunny, tree filled grounds. The girls who are my minders make me think of the girls in my Bunty magazines. I am sure they all have ballet lessons and own ponies. I feel utterly and totally overwhelmed and can barely speak. I am not sure if it is the wheelchair or the social class which creates the biggest barrier, but I do not long to back there. Even the nice girls who do dutifully visit me for several months make me feel uncomfortable. I am not really a friend but their charity case. I play Beatles music to them very loudly on our new record player. "She loves you Yeah! Yeah! Yeah!" I sing, but they do not join in. Gradually the visits stop and I cannot even remember their names. I am angry.

Noel Watson

At the age of around ten or eleven I notice a different tone coming into people's voices as they admire my latest drawings. The word 'Illustrator' is spoken of as if that is something good, worthy of respect and maybe "Something you could do at home".

Although my interest in art was originally driven by an intense desire to be creative, all this praise, encouragement and subtle channelling towards a career gradually seeps into my mind and sets a seed. I cannot stop it. I begin to realize that working class people do not really do 'Fine Art' which is what I really love. It is a luxury we cannot afford, like ballet lessons or learning to play the violin. The problem is that it seems like the only thing I can do well.

There is only really one way in which doing 'Art' in our sort of family could be taken seriously and that is if it you might be good enough to use your talent as a way to earn a living. Suddenly this idea takes off in my family. "God closes one door and opens another" my Aunt Therese tells me.

I am not sure whether I am trying to please myself or all these hopeful adults around me, but I start to think of myself as a professional book illustrator getting commissions from publishers and being paid enough money that I could buy all the paper and inks, paints and brushes that my heart desired. People admire artists so I would have a valued place in the world forever.

When the weekly hours of home tuition were upped by the Education Authority from eight to ten, it was suggested that one hour a week of this was used to employ an Art Teacher who might be able to help develop my talents in this possible route to future employment. I do not know how he was found but a local man, slightly famous for his cartoons in the Croydon Advertiser, knocked on our door and offered to take me on. My Mum and Dad are delighted but I am not that sure about the whole thing. He seems less interested in talking to me than in standing in our kitchen talking very animatedly to Mum who looks a bit starstruck. I don't really like his cartoons either.

He teaches me one thing that changed my style of drawing in a very positive way. He says I don't have to do all the drawing in the middle of the paper leaving a white border all around. He says I could draw right up to the edges, filling the space as though the edge of the paper was a window frame through which I am looking. He makes me look through the window and notice that what I can see may include only part of something like half a tree. Even if I didn't draw the whole tree, the brain of whoever was looking at it would fill in the rest of the tree with their imagination.

He brings in books with the drawings of Aubrey Beardsley who took the beauty of black and white graphic design to a level I had never seen before. He implies that my style is similar and could be improved to his standard, and Beardsley was famous in the illustrating world, therefore my logic takes me, I could become famous. To encourage me further he takes one of my drawings away with him to see if he could convince the editors of the Croydon Advertiser to publish it in the 'local artists' spot, which they do, even though I am only 12.

My teacher Noel Watson talks to me about going to Art College when I am older, but there is a problem with this idea that everyone is quick to point out. I would need 2 A levels and a portfolio of work in order to pass an interview and get accepted to such a hallowed place. I however am an invalid who doesn't go to school. It is out of the question. Quite how they think I am then to become a professional illustrator, even if 'working from home', remains an unspoken mystery.

My future starts to look very dark. I do love painting but I love a lot of other things too. The blinding flash in the garden makes me feel I have to fight very hard to overcome the weight of the appalling history that people like me had had to endure. Earning money seems like the only way anyone gets a life of their own, but how am I going to do that?

My Cousins Take Me in Hand

At around the age of eleven or twelve my bones seem to be getting stronger partly because of the use of my Dad's walking frame. The fractures gradually stop, as long as I am reasonably careful. My Auntie Marcelle, mother of the two cousins Fifi and Billy who grew up in army barracks in Germany, takes what seems like a brave decision. She is the first adult to invite me to stay in her house, without my parents to 'mind' me.

I am really excited as my cousin Fifi is almost the same age as me but much bigger. She is so big in fact that she can carry me about on her hip. This means freedom from adults and opportunities abounding to get up to things together which are not allowed. Given our completely different past lives, we have an amazing amount in common, including strange ideas of how to have fun.

Her brother Billy is even older and stronger. Neither of them pay much attention to the idea that I am the Poor Little Fragile Thing the adults had portrayed. Or maybe they do, but just love to frighten me enough to make me scream and laugh. We run along the banks of the river with Billy pushing me fast in my old battered 'push' chair down steep grassy paths, swerving under bridges with one wheel off the ground and over the water, my terrified shouts echoing against the brickwork.

Fifi carries me downstairs at night, whispering and giggling quietly so as not to wake up her parents, as we crawl through the kitchen hatch and slip out of the back door to meet her latest boyfriend at the deserted railway station. I feel I have gone wild, loving every moment.

Luckily for me, they also take it upon themselves to tell me the facts of life. Their army life had given them the sort of education 'nice' girls are not given. Amongst the rude songs about Hitler's Balls and some poor woman's 'Nikinido' they explain to me what sex is and how it is done. Clearly my family do not think I would ever need to know such things, or certainly not for a long time. I am actually quite disgusted by the revelations, especially when it dawns on me that my own parents might be doing it (Yuk!) but I am so glad to be told anyway.

When I start menstruating not much after being given this vital lesson, having not been otherwise prepared in any way, I am very grateful to have some idea that this was a normal thing, and that I was not just bleeding to death.

CHAPTER THIRTEEN

Portals to Rebellion

Radio Caroline

I AM IN BED quite late at night, wide awake but with the light off. Next to my ear is a little black transistor radio. It is tuned to Radio Caroline, a pirate radio station broadcasting illegally from a ship, 'Caroline', moored just out of British controlled seaways. Just listening to it makes me feel I am part of the teenage rebellion which I so long to join. A voice new to me comes on. A strange slightly harsh voice with a compelling guitar accompaniment. It is saying that the 'Times are a-changing'. One verse in particular catches my attention:

"Come Mothers and Fathers throughout the land,
Dont' criticize what you don't understand,
Your sons and your daughters are beyond your command
The old road is rapidly fading,
Please get out of the new one if you can't lend a hand,
Cos the times, they are a-changing".

This is different! His name is Bob Dylan. He is called a folk singer.

Something inside me tingles with excitement. I have discovered a whole world of political singer-songwriters who seem to be saying all is not well with the world, and I am not the only one to feel angry about it. Suddenly I feel I am less alone, less strange. Putting my concerns and feelings into a musical form gives them weight - 'gravitas' - a seriousness of intent. It validates my thinking. I cannot get enough of it.

Somehow I discover more of these wonderful artists and performers - Pete Seeger, Joan Baez, Tom Paxton and our own Donovan. I make long recordings from the radio onto our 4-track reel-to-reel tape recorder and then play them for hours. I begin to sit up until the early hours of the morning listening to 'Tambourine Man' and 'Masters of War'. Everyone else in my house hates these recordings, but I learn many of the words off by heart without even making an effort.

I now cannot imagine my life without these far-away comrades. I buy Woody Guthrie vinyl discs and read about his life which fascinates me because it turned out that he was disabled too. I learn that his mother had Huntingdon's' Chorea, a progressive disease which only appears in middle age. His family protected her in order to keep her out of the 'Madhouse' even though her behaviour became more and more bizarre and dangerous. Woody had inherited this disease and spent many years being cared for by his own family and 'fans'. Like so many of our 'heroes' he was not really famous in his own life-time. I find all this really, really interesting. It seems to give me hope, but hope for what I am not sure.

Discovering Political Protest

At around this age I see a strange black sign painted on a lamp post outside our front garden. It is round with a vertical line and two side-shooting stems making triangles inside the circle. I ask what it is, fascinated. I am told it is the sign of CND, the Campaign for Nuclear Disarmament. Ban the Bomb.

I am afraid of the Bomb. The dropping of the atom bomb on Horishima and Nagasaki is quite recent history (1945) and there is a general fear in society that we are going to blow ourselves up and end the world. This is because there will be World War Three, probably between America and Russia in which this bomb will be used. Our Government now has its' own nuclear weapons and is building nuclear bunkers underground, mainly for themselves. This is so they can maintain 'Command and Control' while the rest of us evaporate. Sometimes these 'secret' bunkers make 'humps' in parks appear which we are not supposed to notice or talk about. I have nightmares about mushroom clouds appearing over Croydon and have learned all the words to 'Masters of War' by Bob Dylan. But I am still a child with no money so do not see how I can really join up. I therefore 'join' in my head and heart, becoming a mini peace activist which mainly consists of drawing CND logos all over the place where they might annoy people.

CHAPTER THIRTEEN

Her Majesty's Inspector Helps Me Escape

THE HMI SCHOOL INSPECTOR sent round once a year to check that my home tuition is real and working, is sitting back in an armchair, sipping his coffee. I am in my place, on the sofa, with my dutiful Mr Stone sitting beside me, looking scholarly. The Inspector suddenly turns to me and looks me in the eye, an act by which I am a bit startled, so unusual it was. "Tell me" he says "Aren't you bored here at home all the time?" I resisted the urge to scream "YES!!" whilst flinging myself round his neck. Instead I returned his gaze for quite a long, silent time and then shyly agreed that things were not really going my way.

I am 13 years old, the year 1964. I have a one-point-plan to get accepted into Art College, but know that to do so I will need to have taken, and passed, two A levels, and to produce a portfolio of promising work. This latter I can imagine doing even whilst trapped at 141 Limpsfield Road, but the taking of O levels and A levels at home is not possible. Does this man-saviour have an idea in mind? He starts to mutter about a new school about to open designed especially for brainy disabled girls like me. He then seems to think he should go and talk to my parents before putting too much hope into my heart. He stands up and disappears into the kitchen where they are both lurking. Mr Stone begins to turn into his namesake, but I am much too excited to notice the impact this new development might have on him.

Later that day, after both men had gone and my parents had had some time to digest the proposal, we sit down together to have a serious talk.

The Inspector had told my parents the story of how the Treloar project started in 1907 when the then Lord Mayor of the City of London, Sir William Purdie Treloar, set up a 'Cripples' Fund' as his mayoral appeal. His aim was to build a hospital and school outside the city for children with impairments and chronic illnesses. In 1908, Sir William opened his school and hospital in Alton, Hampshire. There, disabled boys were treated for long term impairments mostly resulting from the big polio outbreak in the 1950's. The children's wards, as was common in those days, morphed into sheltered workshops in which the boys were trained in useful skills, primarily mending radio sets, and manufacturing surgical boots. Some then left the institution and went off to something like a 'normal' life, earning their own living, getting married and so on.

The daughter of the Lord Mayor, Florence Treloar, had this radical idea that some disabled girls might also benefit from an education. At this time no special school in the country offered a curriculum which equalled that found in mainstream schools, even less found in Grammar schools. "Surely" she thought "The girls should be given a chance too".

She founded a charity school - The Florence Treloar Grammar School for Disabled (Handicapped) girls. It was in Holybourne, near Alton in Hampshire, about two miles away from the boy's school. Of course, it was a boarding school, but for the first time in the UK a few young disabled women would be given the opportunity to study for public examinations including A levels.

The Inspector told my parents that I had already passed their entrance requirements by passing my 11+. If I wanted to go, we could apply for a full Local Authority grant which he said would be successful. It was a 'special' school yes, but not like any other. What did I think?

For me there was little choice. Did I want to spend the rest of my years parked on our sofa listening to Mrs Dale's Diary with my Mummy, or did I want a life? The goal was Art College and this was the way to achieve it. I said I wanted to go. My parents, especially my Mum, were not thrilled. I do not think they had ever envisaged any sort of leaving on my part, especially before I was even fourteen, nor did they really believe it would lead to a future out in the world for me. They harboured fears that the real adult world was competitive and cruel and the sooner I accepted this the better for me. However, although I could read all this doubt on their faces, they only put up very weak verbal arguments to counter my determination, all of which I demolished like coconuts on a shy. The decision was made to accept the offer and plans began to be made. This included a visit and an interview at the school itself even whilst it was still under construction.

Dressing Up

When the letter arrives announcing my acceptance to Florence Treloar's, it comes with a shopping list. For the first time in my life I am going to have to wear a school uniform. My new boarding school was imagined, organised, funded and staffed by members of the Owning Class. They seemed determined to make ladies of us despite our wheelchairs and whatnots. I doubt that it occurred to them that their local authority sponsored families had never heard of 'Gorringe's' or might struggle to pay Gorringe prices for such a bespoke set of clothes. Clearly, we have no choice.

We make a special trip into London (by which we meant everything north of the river Thames) to be measured for the individually made set of summer and winter outfits, complete with straw boater and grey felt hat. The design follows a colour scheme of grey and green with checked cotton dresses for the Summer, and the most extraordinary flapped grey cross-over skirt for the winter months. I think it had all been specially designed with ease of dressing in mind. I am both fascinated and horrified by it all. "Thank God" I think "No one I know is ever going to see me dressed up in this lot". No more jeans and Sloppy Joes for me. No more make-up and back to pristine white socks. The tininess of my feet still poses a problem for school shoes so a concession is made to allow me to carry on wearing my own shoes, despite their pointed toes. In fact, when the summer dresses arrive, they do not really work on my unusual frame and my Mum is allowed to buy similar material and make some smock-like version which is more wearable for me. Every item has to have a name-tag sewn in by hand. Even this name-tag was posh, having had to order a length of tape with my name actually woven into it. We didn't know such stuff existed. "What is wrong with indelible pens on bias - binding" we muttered whilst stitching away at this onerous task.

Eventually the suitcase is packed with the listed items, all ready to accompany me into a new stage of life. The name tapes and the hats are already making me feel that I am entering into a play someone else had written. I was to become an actress on a different stage. This new stage was where opportunity existed, where I could be prepared to take my place on the world stage as long as I played my part correctly. The danger would be allowing my audience to see that really, I was just a working-class imposter wearing dressing up clothes and speaking my lines in a false accent. Could I fool them?

Did I Kill Mr Stone?

There is something not right with my teacher Mr Stone. He seems to be shrinking, or fading and I am concerned that it is something to do with the fact that he is not going to be teaching me for much longer.

Before he came to me Mr Stone had been widowed. His wife Geraldine was the love of his life and he had not got over the loss. He has children and at least one grandchild, but does not see them very often. He also misses being a Headteacher about which he speaks often. I had been told by him, and my parents, that coming to our house three times a week had given him something to live for.

He begins to take days off and the word cancer is mentioned. He looks like he is in pain, especially when sitting down and getting up, but he never speaks to me about this. I am used to being able to talk to him about most things and I am sure I carried on talking about going to Boarding School, and the hope of having friends of my own age. "Just promise me one thing" he says, "That you will stay as sweet as you are now". I do not feel very 'sweet' and don't know how to answer him. I look down and keep on drawing.

The next day he does not turn up. Nor the next. After a few more of these days my Dad comes into the living room in his Uniform having received a phone call at the Station (we do not have a phone of our own) and says he has sad news. Mr Stone has died. I am afraid that it was me who has killed him, taking away his lifeline. I do not take in any more information – how my family reacted to the news – but slip off the sofa and go upstairs to my bedroom. I refuse to talk about it to anyone for many years.

CHAPTER FOURTEEN

The Treloar Experiment

I AM NOT WORRIED about going to a place full of disabled people whilst I am awake. The fears come in dreams where half human, half monster children line the corridors making sounds that chill my blood. Half-forgotten memories of real children I had seen when much younger whose heads had swelled to twice their normal size due to untreated hydrocephalus floated now into my vision. I know that I am one of them but this knowledge terrifies me. I wake early, relief flooding my body as the nightmare fades into the familiar colours and shapes of my bedroom in the early morning light. It is September 1965, the first day of the first term of the new school opening its doors to the carefully picked first band of young women who would fill the long corridors, the dormitories, the classrooms, swimming pool, science lab, art rooms, dining hall with a living experiment in equal opportunities.

The school had to be filled with every age of pupil catered for, from eleven years old to past eighteen. Many girls had been identified by their various special schools as bright, bored and in need of stretching academically, but a good number had been excluded from mainstream schools. The excuse they used seemed to be mostly that their impairment-related needs, for example getting from classroom to classroom loaded down by heavy books, was becoming a problem they would rather someone else sorted out.

A small group of older students had left special school without any qualifications and therefore had found themselves almost unemployable. They had chosen to come into the 6th form to take up the chance to get O and A levels and then possibly, go on to University. An even smaller group of pupils had been sent overseas from the 'Commonwealth' to help boost the numbers and make the school as a whole a viable option. There were about forty pupils altogether, about half of the schools' actual capacity. This means that in each year group, there is only a handful of children. I will be going into the fourth form as I am nearly fifteen. I am one of four.

We pack my labelled dressing-up clothes with some of my ordinary clothes and other belongings into the car, get in with them and set off on the fifty-mile journey down the A3, past Guilford and on down to Alton in Hampshire. None of us can speak. I am full of nervous anticipation and my parents do not seem happy, although they are trying to be cheerful. We find the turn-off to Holybourne, the village in which the school is located, turning left into a quarter-mile drive through an impressive pillared entrance. Carved into stone on the right- hand side is the name 'Florence Treloar Grammar School for Handicapped Girls'. We pass the house where the Headmistress will live with her partner, some other outbuildings then pull up outside the back entrance.

There are many other cars full of families just like mine. Their heads all look normal sized, and a surprising amount of the new pupils don't look disabled at all. Most of them, like me, look like they have no idea what is ahead of them.

We are all surveying the scene for potential friends. Making friends is the first, essential need to be met, or survival in this foreign land will not be possible. I am so distracted by this burning mission that I barely notice my pale-faced Mum and my resolute-faced Dad saying goodbye and driving off. Kindness to adults is not on my mind.

Friends At Last

I am sitting on the toilet behind one of the strangely designed double doors which don't quite close, leaving my dropped knickers exposed to the eyes of anyone who peers closely enough through the gap in the middle. This is taking me some time to get used to. A melodious voice from the stall next door breaks the silence. "Micheline" she says in a strong welsh accent, "Do you think you will ever get married?" All of a sudden, I knew fourteen years of isolation were over. Someone else in this world had grown up facing similar struggles, having similar worries and had been washed up on the same beach as me. "Fuck knows" I thought in my head, but said the same thing a bit more politely to the voice next door which I recognised as belonging to Yvonne.

Many of us had spent our first few days at our new school standing back and observing the extraordinary collection of young people who were to be our fellow inmates for the next few years. Who seemed to be potential friends, who seemed to be people to avoid, who seemed to be too young, too old, or too strange to warrant the effort of getting to know – all needed to be worked out. But for me there was an obvious choice, a sense of a natural gravitational pull towards three girls, all from the same special school in South Wales.

Their parents are all involved in the Steel works in Port Talbot. On the surface they are very different to one another – Yvonne is a polio survivor with long chestnut hair and beautiful green eyes, made for flirting; Theresa is a natural comic with a fixed unbending hip as a result of some surgery aimed at easing her arthritic pain; Lindy is round and buxom with blond hair and a piercing intellect. She has a form of brittle bones but not OI, so can walk for at least some of the time. They are all funny and full of life and, despite the differences, they share a down-to-earth solidity that I find very attractive.

They know each other well so they are less overwhelmed by the unfamiliarity of our new environment than most of us. I am drawn to them and hope they will let me be part of their gang. I don't know if the Matron who had decided how to allocate the beds in our dormitories was really astute about social class, but she puts us together in that first term and it made becoming friends much easier. In fact, I soon start talking with a welsh accent myself in some sort of compulsive fitting-in phenomena. I have to apologise for this quite often, especially when asked what it is like coming to England for the first time.

The main thing we share is our ability to make each other laugh. I did not know until then that when given the right sort of peer group I could turn almost any of life's difficulties, or irrationalities, into a comedy script. I also did not forsee that I would meet other young people like me who could do the same. Consequently, we spent every spare minute doubled up with laughter. Staff are unsurprisingly irritated by this, especially late at night when we are supposed to be sleeping, not playing volleyball in the dark and breaking things.

School rules are a shock to me. I had been abandoned to my own devices for my whole childhood. If I didn't make my own decisions about what to do next, I would have evaporated out of boredom. If I hadn't read almost every book in Sanderstead Lending Library, and worked out how to use this second-hand information to think about life, I would not be able to direct my own life and would become a complete victim of circumstances.

At fourteen I feel it is too late to expect me to start following orders without weighing them up in my own mind first. I ask "Why?" too many times. It doesn't take long before the staff in the school start seeing me as a problem child. I am told I have the Wrong Attitude, but I don't really know what they mean.

The staff force me to wear their peculiar grey and green clothing although much of it, including the six-foot-long scarf, looks ridiculous on me. I rebel and put purple tinsel in my shoes instead of laces. Is this what they mean? It turns out that many of the hand-picked first cohort of pupils had been identified by their special schools as trouble makers. This included my welsh gang of frustrated teenagers, joking about everything but fuelled by a deep vein of anger at the mistreatment and discrimination they had all experienced.

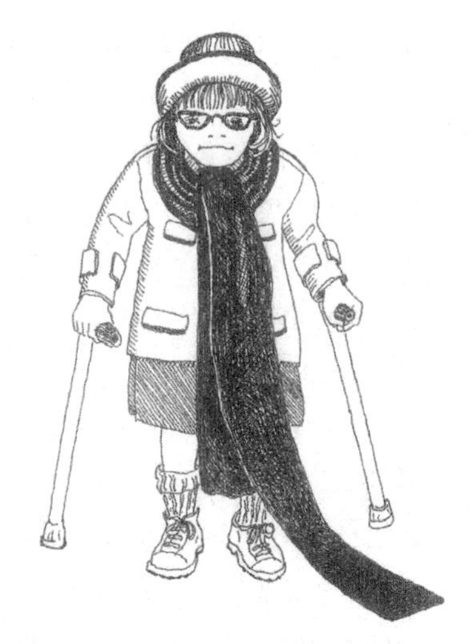

Modelling my 6' uniform scarf

As much as the expectation of conformity is a shock to me, the reality of the energy, non-conformity and determination to 'get a life' bursting out of their new pupils is a shock to the innocent staff who it seems were expecting something more passive, like grateful dollies in wheelchairs, than the semi delinquent bunch we turn out to be.

There are no rules when we first arrive at the school but very quickly there are long lists of things we must not do, written up and strictly enforced. We create them by our 'bad' behaviour. To me the most bizarre are the ones about how we must behave outside the school grounds. We must not go out without a member of staff. We must walk in 'crocodiles' two or three abreast in straight lines along the pavement. We must always wear school uniform including hats. We must request any outing at least three days in advance.

Gradually a substantial number of the pupils, including those who had entered at sixth form level, amalgamate into a resistance movement. Led by the older girls we demand a meeting with staff at which, to their amazement, we explain the difficulties with their notions of how to manage us, spelling out what agreements we are willing to make with them. The learning curve for them is so steep they need nails in their boots to prevent them from sliding off, whilst I experience for the first time in my life the delicious feeling of collective power.

The crocodiles are never seen again straddling the too-narrow pavements of the astonished village of Holybourne. Instead we have the simple rule that we must always go out in packs of three or more *(one person to have an accident, one person to stay with the victim, one person to go for help)* to be recorded in a clocking-in-and-out book. Weekends only.

Catching the Bus

Some of us cannot wait to get out and explore our nearby towns, all of which are a bus or train ride away. I have never been on either without my parents. The local bus drivers have no idea what is to befall them.

Any outing begins with getting down our quarter of a mile drive without a bus to help. As I am coming to expect my welsh friends have a wonderful solution to this problem. We all get into wheelchairs, even those who don't need them, and gather at the top of the drive. Lindy is the brains behind the plan. "Get in line, each one holding the handles of the chair in front of you" she instructs, putting herself at the front as the strongest pusher. Now we are all lined up in a static queue she shouts "We're off!" and starts to use all her strength to get the train moving. It was hard and began slowly, only made possible by the fact that the drive sloped gently downwards towards the entrance. Gradually however we built up speed. Lindy's role changed from power engine to simply steering the rolling mass of slightly terrified girls in a straight line.

Naturally we go faster and faster. Small screams of fear and excitement start to escape from our mouths such as we might make on an accelerating ride at a fun fair. The screams get louder as the speed starts to feel uncontrolled and dangerous, but as we hurtle past the gardener's cottage at the end of the drive, Lindy shouts "Let go!" allowing the chain to splinter into individual chairs the passengers of which have to regain control and stop before any of us shoot out onto the large and busy main road which rumbles along at the foot of the drive. This is easier said than done. Some of us deliberately steer into hedges and walls, but mainly we manage to stay upright and unscathed apart from the friction burns on our hands as we grip the spinning wheels of our chairs to slow them down. I make a mental note to always put myself at the back so I can choose when to let go if I feel it is all getting too fast for my safety. Lindy finds it all very funny.

As we must go out in three 's or more there are quite a number of us traversing the main road to sit and wait at the bus stop for a ride to Alton. Between us we have a varied collection of folding wheelchairs and an assortment of crutches all of which, along with ourselves, have to be got into the bus and then out again at our destination. I am amazed that the bus driver actually stops for us. Maybe he thinks we are just there to wave off the one of us who appears the most 'normal' but it takes only a minute for him to realise what a mistake he has made.

Clambering on, propping ourselves up with bars and the tops of seats – maybe the arm of an unsuspecting passenger – we all manage to get aboard, dragging our equipment behind us. It takes ten minutes or more. The drivers face is turning from red to puce. The passengers' eyes are round as saucers, gasping with the shock of it. The bus pulls off. I think the driver is quietly shaking. We don't care. We are triumphantly on our way! It is amazing what I will do with other people – things I would never contemplate on my own.

We all disembark at a bus stop in the middle of town, much to the relief of our hostage driver and passengers. There are all the usual shops, pubs, churches, and so on. We find to our delight an open door with a juke box inside, the wonderful 'Rendevous Cafe'. We pour in, settle down at several tables and pool our small amount of cash to buy coke, chips and endlessly feed the juke box, a common attraction in the 1960s. The noise level in the café goes up by about a hundred decibels but it seems we are welcome. As usual we are laughing about everything. The locals are stunned. We are definitely not what they were expecting when they signed the petition to refuse planning permission for the 'Institution' unless it was set back a quarter of a mile from the road and behind a substantial brick wall.

Complaints were made. The bus drivers contacted the school regaling them with the horrors of our invasion of the public transport system. The public doesn't include us it seems. Matron gives us a stern talking to. She makes us acknowledge that holding up a bus for fifteen minutes is very inconsiderate of the other passengers. We were to divide ourselves up into groups of three and limit ourselves to one group per bus. As busses were not that frequent in our little village, this did cause us difficulties meeting up at the Rendevous Café 'en masse' and also getting back on time. We have to take into account the push-back up the long school drive which was such fun on the outward journey with gravity on our side, but nothing but a long slog on the uphill journey. However, it doesn't stop us.

The Train Ride

Train journeys bring different challenges. We are intrigued by the idea of getting to a further destination – Farnham or

Winchester – on our own by train. How can it be done? Three of us set off to find out. I am the only wheelchair user. We get by bus to the nearest railway station and ask for three tickets to our chosen destination. As a younger child I had travelled on the train with my family but then I had been carried on by my Dad and sat in the carriage with everyone else. My chair, if we bought it at all, had to be folded and stored on the luggage rack. Now as an independent teenage traveller, clearly something else would need to happen.

Several men in British Rail uniforms arrived to deal with me. Nothing is accessible so the adventure begins by being escorted to the end of the platform, through a 'No One Past This Point' gate, half pushed half carried over bumpy railway tracks (Isn't one of them electrified?), back through another gate and up to the correct platform to catch the train.

I like this apparent breaking of the rules. It feels exciting. The men are very confident that we will all be safe – not run over or electrocuted. They are like my Fireman Dad I think. However, we are not to get into a carriage with the other passengers. When the train arrives, I am pushed to the end where the guard's van hisses at us. Two men are needed to lift me in my chair up the steps into the gloomy interior. This does not feel so safe. Once put down and brakes applied I look around the large space with slight horror. There are no seats. My friends who had insisted that we stay together were offered a crate of smelly fish to sit on. In the far dark corner yellow eyes gleam and a low growling reach my ears. Dogs with muzzles are our companions. We are luggage, not real passengers at all!

The guard sits in with us, chatting away as the train rumbles off. As the speed builds up and the carriage begins to rock he has to keep hold of my chair so I do not slide around the floor. We are all giggling nervously, now suppressing a growing concern about getting off the train at the other end. Was someone going to be there to help lift me down those steep steps?

On arrival more uniformed men do appear, much to my relief. I am very small and light as teenagers go, so can be carried in my chair by two competent people. We are quick to realise that bigger, heavier school mates would be taking much more of a risk, not to mention the risk to the backs of the staff who had to move us around without any ramps or lifts to help. It also takes an age. Our total journey is only two or three stops, but nevertheless when we get there we have to catch the next train back in order to comply with our strict curfew.

I am a bit shocked by it all, especially the fish and the dogs, but again we had done it and lived to see another day. However, the sense of being second class passengers whilst paying the same fare as everyone else burns deep within us.

CHAPTER FIFTEEN

Knuckling Down

ONE OF THE MAIN differences between our school and mainstream secondary schools is that when the hour is up at the end of the lesson, instead of a thousand young people standing up, gathering books, pens and personal belonging, moving out into the corridors to set off on the long journey up and down stairs to find the correct classroom for the next lesson, we all stay put at our desks and the teachers move round. Even Miss Watson who is herself disabled simply stacks all her books onto a trolley and pushes it to her next class. It all seems so simple to me, not having experienced anything else.

The exceptions are the lessons which require a lot of specialist equipment – Art, Science, domestic science and music. All these have their own rooms including sound-proofed piano booths for practicing our scales. We even have our own heated swimming pool which I love. I am amazed that all this stuff was just for us. The all-age special school in Croydon to which we all decided I should not go, certainly didn't have anything like it.

It slowly dawns on me that if we are to be offered the opportunity to take O and A levels then they are obliged to provide the environment in which this could happen. I am especially excited at the science lab with its gas Bunsen burners and all sort of glass test tubes, jars and chemicals. 'Physics', another subject taught alongside science, was a new word to me. What is it? Will I get to learn something completely new? Unfortunately, I am told it was not to be.

I am not asked what I want to study at my new school. My curriculum is designed by the staff and presented to me as a demand. I have come to Treloar's with a very limited back-story of subjects taught. I am clearly good at Art and English Literature having devoured every book and comic I could get my hands on. I had drawn my way to fame via the Croydon Advertiser, so it was decided I should take these two O levels early, at fifteen, leaving more space and time to catch up and take exams in the other subjects of which I have only a smattering of experience – maths, history, geography and French – the following year. As I have never done science it Is deemed too late to start now. 'Physics' is to remain a complete mystery to me. Their goal is to get as many of us as possible passing exams in order to prove the Florence Treloar Experiment is working. I am a means two their end. However, my one-point-programme of getting into Art College needs me to have two A levels. If these are to be Art and English I am not complaining, so I just get on with it.

Apart from Art and English Literature with their exceptionally good teachers, I find many of the lessons intensely boring. Until now I have not experience sitting at a desk for a whole hour whilst a teacher demands my attention. One-to-one home tuition had to some degree given me a privileged learning experience, albeit it in a very narrow field, as it was much more of a two-way thing. During the rest of my days I had taught myself through reading, watching people and cajoling my parents to let me have a go at whatever they were doing whether it was rolling pastry or wiring a plug.

Practical skills I had picked up through trial and error, experimenting with toys, kits and art and craft materials. As no one was watching or judging me, it was a good way to learn. I learned how to do things right by doing them wrong first. This is the best way in my view as I internalised the whole experience, understanding exactly why things need to be done a certain way to succeed. I knew that if I didn't knot my cotton the stitches would come undone. I knew that if I mixed yellow paint with blue paint I would get green, not brown. I knew that if I dropped a knitting stitch and didn't pick it up straight away, I would find a 'ladder' down the whole length of my garment. Now I have to adjust to something completely different and I do not find it easy.

Studying history is a particular problem because I seem to have an unconscious block towards the subject the way it is taught. I am suspicious of it as it is not my history as a working-class person, and even less as a disabled person. The Tudors and Stuarts, the Battle of Balaclava and the creation of the British Empire are of no interest to me at all. I cannot see how they relate to life as I know it. I get very low marks for my scribbled too-short essays but I have no words to explain my difficulty.

Maths is a different problem. I had been good at the subject at home having benefited from the mental wrestling matches with my dear Mr Stone. His death had caused me a great deal of pain, particularly as I felt guilty for being so enthusiastic about leaving him to come to this school. As usual I do not think there is anyone I can talk to about all this. It just festers in my heart and clogs up my brain. I do not think I learn anything new mathematically speaking after our relationship came to its abrupt end. The new maths teacher tries his best but it is the only O' level subject which I fail.

Cramming

At school I discover the art of cramming. I am good at it. For a few days before an exam I get up in the very early hours of the morning to sit in the deserted library with a lovely hot cup of coffee. There I notate everything I might be asked to produce in the exam, get out my books and past essays and commit to my short-term memory everything I think I might be asked to regurgitate onto the paper. This data stays in my brain for about ten milliseconds after I pour it as best I can onto the correct Official Sheet after which I deleted it. If I had been asked to repeat this performance the following day I don't think anything much would have been written. I have already cleared my mental decks for all the stuff I really want to learn and to be able to recall for my own purposes. I do not think I am alone in this, and it makes me start to wonder about this thing called a 'State Education' – who is it really for?

Civics, or Learning How the World Works.

Some lessons however will stay with me forever. We are getting out of our school bus and take a deep breath. "Oh my God it stinks!" wails Theresa. "I am going to be sick" announces a pale-green faced Jenny, clutching a handkerchief to her nose and mouth. It is a field trip to our local sewage works. We are all in our grey and white summer uniform dresses complete with green cardigans but without boaters or gas masks.

I am fascinated. We are taken on a tour of the huge circular tanks where the waste from our toilets and drains on the streets tumble down long, hidden underground pipes to reappear here in their raw and smelly state. They pass through an amazing system where living microbes digest the solid matters transforming them eventually into clean water. More pipes then take the treated water out to the nearest rivers where we are told it joins our natural waterways without doing any harm to the fish or birds.

Like most people I have not given a lot of thought to what happens when I flush. I am not aware that there are places like this everywhere around the country. We all contaminate water and a whole battalion of people have to clean it up for us. Who else works behind the scenes to make our world work? I have grown up with a Dad who works for public services. I can see that the fire engines he drives are very loud and visible, and the people who man them are almost public heroes, but now I am becoming aware that many other people do vital community work out of sight and, except to their families perhaps, out of mind too.

Reading about it would not have made the profound impact that the visit made, assaulting our senses and witnessing the transformation in person. I am looking forward to drawing the diagrams and am sorry that I will not be allowed to embellish them with pictures of Jenny throwing up, or our tour guide with his glass of treated sewage proudly saying "Here, drink this!"

The School Journey

The school bus is loaded - a Royal Variety Sunshine Coach. Two rows of girls in wheelchairs facing each other line the back half of the large vehicle. Down the middle is a third row facing forwards. None of us are clamped or strapped into place. Our safety depends on the effectiveness of our own brakes and the fact that we are jammed in so tightly there is not much room to move about. There is luggage also, stuffed into the racks above our heads.

Between us and the driver there are a few rows of seats for the walking members of the group.

We are all very excited and talking loudly without doing much listening. Nerves are being hidden by staff, pupils and the reckless parents who have seen fit to support this venture.

Maybe they are just desperate for a break. Whatever the reason, we are going to drive to Holland!

Mr Breckin is our school driver whom we all love because he is so funny. He endlessly tells repetitive jokes or sighs "Once a Treloar Girl, always a Lady" every time one of us swears or burps. We trusted him with our lives as he drives the long journey to the ferry in which we all sail happily across the North Sea. Most of us have never done anything so adventurous before, especially without the protection of our vigilant parents.

When we actually arrive in the Netherlands however, it seems his usual level of control is being challenged. A Dutchman, our new guide, insists that we follow him around in his own, much smaller vehicle. The problem is that he drives much too fast for us in our large overloaded bus. Mr Breckin is torn between keeping us safe and keeping up with our leader - getting lost in this foreign land is not a good prospect. As we turn right all the chairs lined up on the right-hand side begin to slide to the left. When we turn left those of us seated on the left start to slide to the right. When we have to brake too hard the row in the middle starts to slide forwards whilst we all grab them to try and stop them tumbling over the edge of the raised floor into the sunken seated area. The remaining luggage on the racks starts to fall off onto our heads and laps. We are giggling and shouting "Woah!" but actually starting to feel scared. When we finally screech to a halt outside the Land Reclamation Exhibition we had been bought to see by our oblivious tour-master, we are mightily relieved. Hearing that the Netherlands is mostly below sea level and could obviously therefore be flooded at any time, makes us feel that the Dutch people are living in a strangely insecure world and maybe like danger.

Everywhere we go on our trip people gather from nowhere to stand and watch with amazement as we disembark from our bus on the tail lift. We decide that as we cannot avoid being such an unusual spectacle we will act like celebrities, waving and smiling at our audience who, luckily, could not understand what we were really saying behind the false smiles.

We continue on our journey, careering round Rotterdam, visiting the Delft Factory where beautiful blue and white pottery is made, watch huge cheeses being rolled along the street at a cheese market, and drive along a dyke at the Zeiderzee, or 'Southern Sea'. Here the man-made dyke along which we travel has created a huge fresh water lake on one side, with the sea on the other. The scale has to be seen to be believed as it seems as though we are driving through the sea itself in our little sunshine bus.

We find this very interesting, but nowhere near as interesting as discovering chips stalls open at midnight, served in paper cones with mayonnaise. More than once we put clothes over pyjamas and sneak out from our hostel to buy some. The Dutch boys who seemed to gather round these nocturnal havens of deliciousness, were apparently happy to let us flirt with them in our incomprehensible English. This is the real highlight of the trip.

Mr Brekin eventually refuses to risk our lives any more having damaged our bus rounding a bend which was too narrow. An argument ensues which he wins, parting company from the speedy gentleman. From then on we follow our own maps and timetable and complete our studies before returning home all in one piece. Half the population of the Netherlands it seems come to wave us off at the Ferry Terminal.

CHAPTER SIXTEEN

Sailing Off in My Cripship

IF MY GOAL OF Art College is to be reached, I need to learn how to drive. There are several boys from our 'brother' school the Lord Mayor Treloar College who arrive as visitors to our school in their blue three-wheeled invalid carriages. Although designed for one person, when the sliding door is pushed back it is not unusual for hidden passengers to uncurl from their cramped position on the floor and clatter onto the ground of our car park with various crutches and folding wheelchairs. They are my inspiration. They call their vehicles 'Cripships'. They are issued free of charge by the Government to any disabled person deemed able to pass their driving test primarily so we can get to work unaided. They have two-stroke petrol engines and a tiller bar rather than a steering wheel. This means they can be classified as motorcycles, not cars at all. Consequently, we can drive them at sixteen on a motorcycle licence, something I am keen to do.

You have to know the history of mobility aids for the 'handicapped' to understand how this came about. Originating as basket chairs the first adaptation was the addition of levers to allow the stronger–armed user to turn the wheels independently by pulling and pushing themselves along. When it rained the owner got wet so hoods were added like large prams. Eventually electric motors were added which made it easier to go long distances. This was in turn completely encased in a blue fibre-glass skin with a petrol engine replacing the electric motor. However tinny, noisy and limited these apparitions are, I want one. How else am I to escape 141 Limpsfield Road and get out anywhere by myself?

Now I am soon to be sixteen I find out how to apply for one and for the necessary provisional driving licence. No adults in my life seem to think this is a good idea. When I run the idea before my Mum her face takes on the look of a saddened nurse in a psychiatric hospital listening to a patient who thinks she is the reincarnation of Joan of Arc. "But where on earth would you go dear?" she asks me in complete astonishment. I am reminded of my parents' inability to imagine my future life outside of their house and I don't bother looking to my Dad for encouragement. It is too risky given that I am full of fears of my own which need contradicting, not reinforcing. Didn't they realise I had no choice? My friends at school are more positive given that many of them were busy doing the same thing as me.

Eventually a letter arrives responding to my request. They have made an appointment to be assessed for a possible vehicle at Irene House in Balham, London. They even offer transport to the place which is lucky because I am not sure any of the miserable doom–mongering jailors who run my life would be willing to take me.

I cannot remember if I make this journey from home or school, alone or with friends. They send an ambulance for me which is embarrassing. To me Irene House seems a very important place in the centre of the Big Exiting City which Balham represents. It turns out to be surprisingly small and dingy, but I am still very apprehensive and awestruck.

I do not take a wheelchair on this visit as I can now walk a fair way using elbow crutches. I do not know if this adds to the first reaction of my assessors who seem horrified that anyone so small could be thinking of driving one of their precious motorised tricycles.

I have noticed before that the reality of my three-foot-two-inch stature seems more obvious when I am standing on the floor in an upright position than when I am seated in a wheeled seat raised off the floor. It is an optical illusion not working in my favour. "Ooh you are so small!" they exclaim. Many people in my life have been compelled to point this out to me as if I might be unaware of it without their shattering insight. It is probably only their polite restraint which stops them getting a mirror to show me that I look like some sort of fairy, not the ordinary person I seem to think I am.

As the assessment continues, asking me to squeeze this and pull that, so does their muttering: "Well, they can only say no"; "Not really strong enough", and "I suppose we could try her in a Barratt". I have no idea what a Barratt is, but it sounds better than "Forget it Twinkle".

I am confounded by the logic which seems to imply that the size of the vehicle must be relative to the size of the driver. I am aware that most people are not weighed and measured before being allowed to try an Aston Martin or a Morris Minor in a regular car showroom. And what about those twelve stone weaklings being allowed to drive enormous articulated lorries all over the place? "I am going to drive the bloody thing" I think, "Not carry it!".

I return home confused as to whether I have been successful or not. I hear nothing further. I return to school with a big worry that my plans were being mysteriously foiled behind my back, and this worry stays with me during many months of silence from the adults around me. Despite this, the little word 'Barratt' continues to emit a small glimmer of hope in my heart.

One day a year later when I am seventeen, one of the grounds men in the school announces he has something to show me. He asks me to follow him outside, around the grounds to some out-of-sight garages. My heart starts to beat faster. What is this? He takes me over to a particular garage, unlocks it and says "There. It is yours." Shining in the gloom of its little house is a tiny, green, soft-topped, three-wheeled answer to my prayers. This is a Barratt!

I stroke it. I walk round it. I look inside at the single seat, the tiller bar with the motorbike-like twist grip and clutch, at the gear stick with its notched housing, and at the ignition just waiting for its key. I smell the faint odour of petrol and engine oil overpowering the musty scent of the garage inside which this treasure had been locked for such a long time. My eyes are round as saucers. Here is the mechanical friend which is going to give me my freedom. How long has it been hidden here without my knowledge? Months and months apparently.

I discover that Irene House Officials had written to my parents as I was a minor (under 21 in those days) to express their concern about my size and age. Together with my Headmistress they had conspired to make me wait a year to see if I would 'grow up' in all the ways they thought I hadn't. I am not as angry about this as I often am when I feel the stupid adults are conspiring against children in general, and me in particular. The truth is I am very scared at the thought of driving. I have not had a single word of encouragement from anyone and a history of fragility and broken bones. I am not at all sure I will be able to safely control this powerful machine, follow the rules of the road and avoid tipping it or crashing it, possibly killing self and others. It is just that I have to try or be condemned to a life time of imprisonment. And anyway, Lindy can do it, so why not me?"

The Barratt comes as part of a package complete with a very limited number of driving lessons and a copy of the Highway Code. I am to have my lessons whilst still at school. It is thought that the quiet country lanes would be a safe place for me and all the other pupils who wanted to learn to drive to practice. This was not really fully thought out because our school was built on the North Downs. The roads were narrow, steep and edged with deep nettle-filled ditches on both sides. When another vehicle – often a huge farm machine – is met in the lane it means crawling behind it in a very low gear, or trying to pass it by nearly tipping into the deadly ditches which are malevolently waiting for our wobbly little motorised crates to fall in and swallow up.

Officially, being classed as a motor cycle, the driving instructor is meant to teach us from the roadside, showing us how to get moving before sending us off round the block until we hopefully return in one piece. If we succeed in this he leans through the window to give further instructions. My instructor did not do this.

Having helped me get into the little vehicle and to familiarise myself with its controls he climbs in next to me, sitting on the floor by my side. His weight, twice that of mine at least, then tips the whole vehicle to the left. This means that I have to exert a lot more strength on the tiller bar just to keep my Barratt moving in a straight line. It also makes it harder to put on the brake requiring me to lean with all my strength and weight in order to put a downward pressure on the tiller bar. Sometimes he has to help me which doesn't seem right.

Changing gear is also problematic in that in that I have to let go of the tiller bar with my right hand in order to move the gear stick, but also need the combined strength of both arms to steer the thing. I learn eventually to use a foot to kick it into gear when necessary. The unfortunate thing is that I try to avoid changing gear because it is so difficult, chugging along in a cloud of petrol fumes in second gear when I should be breezing along in fourth. Quite frankly I am terrified.

In a sweaty, rigid state I am persuaded by my overconfident instructor to start up the engine, pull in the clutch, pull the gear stick into first, open the throttle and move off. Why he is not deafened by my pounding heart I do not know. Maybe he is too concerned with his own. I get the feel of the steering and practice a few stops and starts. Then he tells me to drive right through the back entrance with our face-painted concrete balls (Lindy and I had embellished these 'finials' with black paint one bored Sunday afternoon) onto the country lane leading into the wilderness of the Holybourne countryside.

Our journey is painstakingly slow, but I do not panic. We grind up a few hills and manage to steer round the bends without ending up in the ditch. Eventually my instructor asks me to drive into the bumpy entrance of a farmyard where I turn the vehicle around for the homeward journey. Killing my speed is topmost in my mind but it starts to irritate my instructor. He tells me I am doing OK and to let it go a bit faster. I think he is mad but do what he asks. Somehow, I manoeuvre the downhill bends without any deaths occurring. I am so relieved to see those balls and the lovely flat, ditchless roads of our school grounds that I actually start to breathe normally. "Well done!" he says. I want to kiss him.

The Diaspora

In my final year I take and pass the vital A levels, my passport to Art college and my three-year term is over. I have very mixed feelings about leaving school. It is a Diaspora of disabled young women who had become very close and learned more from each other than we ever learned from our school curriculum. Boarders like us are forced to disperse when term ends to many far-flung destinations with no certainty we will ever see each other again. Most of us do not have communities of friends back home as we have been victims of segregation, sent away from our local schools and homes for most of the time.

However different to each other we are as Treloar girls, we are all in agreement on one thing – we should never have been segregated from the mainstream into a special school, and we are not going to remain in a disabled ghetto one minute longer than necessary. We are certain that disability needs to be understood as a normal part of the human condition, and those of us who have them need to be included in every aspect of life. This means going out into the 'able-bodied' world and carving a place for ourselves in it, almost like foreigners in our own land. A very daunting task.

For me the isolation of my early childhood is not something I ever want to repeat so I am happy that at least two of my friends from Treloar's live within a few miles of my home in South Croydon, Mary Woodhouse and the beautiful Florence. A third pupil, Nancy Willis becomes another life-long friend.

The Continuing Bonds of Friendship.

Mary

Mary is younger than me so we do not mix educationally. There is a colossal divide in our school between the 'Juniors' and the 'Seniors'. However, she lives less than two miles away from me so we tentatively make arrangements to visit each other during the long school holidays.

Like me she is working class although her Mother is a teacher with 'Upper Working Class' aspirations just like my Mother. Mary and I seem to share the same sense of humour and spend a lot of time giggling about silly things. She plays the piano which I admire having so little musical talent of my own. Her brother also had what was then thought to be muscular dystrophy, later re-diagnosed as spinal muscular atrophy, and I had already met him when I was twelve when we were both (naughty) patients in hospital. They had both suffered being sent at a very early age to special boarding school despite their mother's heroic efforts to keep them in the mainstream. Mary tells me often about the constant fear of the next return to school even when she was trying to enjoy the holiday respite at home. Clearly choosing to get away from home at fourteen as I had done was not at all the same as being sent away from home at the age of five. That I just can't imagine.

Nancy

Nancy comes to our school at about the age of fifteen, an exile from a local mainstream school which had deemed that because of her progressive muscular dystrophy, she had become too unsteady on her feet to be safe in the corridors, awash as they were with a moving sea of fellow students all waiting to knock her over. A safe passage in a wheelchair does not seem to be an option anyone has considered.

She is not happy to have been separated from her friends and sent to special school. She bitterly resents it as far as I can tell. I am a bit in awe of her as she has come from Normal Land and looks cool. She is tall with dark hair and a striking face. She seems to be treated a bit differently than the rest of us, including being allowed to sit in our Matron's office and smoke. I think her anger made her refuse to cooperate with school rules or the process of studying for, or taking exams. I hear that, like me, she wants to be an Artist. I am drawn to her rebellious spirit. She lives in London, not too far from me and I think when I leave school I will try and keep in contact, if she wants.

Florence

Florence may be the friend who most influences my young adult life and I have a lot to thank her for. Florence had come to Treloar's from an all age special school in Wandsworth in order to get enough real education to be able to sit public examinations. I think she was about 15 when we first met. In actual fact, as with Nancy I am so much in awe of her that it is only when we leave that school that we become really close, living within fairly easy reach of each other as we do.

Florence was born in Egypt. Her mother was Italian and her father half French, half Maltese. He was some kind of engineer working for the British Government. When she was three, Florence caught polio and nearly died. The story Florence had been told was that her mother, a devout Catholic, stole her from her hospital bed and took her to a local church where she prayed over her all night. The next morning she started to recover from the fever, but became unable to walk.

Florence recalled sitting on the shoulders of her Ayah, or maid, holding on to her plaits and feeling happy. She went to school with the help of some older girls who were paid to carry her about and take her to the toilet. In school she could speak Italian and French, and was learning to read and write in Arabic. But some political changes, and her father's reaction, led to the whole family having to flee Egypt to come and live in Britain as refugees. Florence repeated the story often of how the family's valuables and papers had been sewn inside her coat lining because they knew the local officials would not touch a disabled child for fear of 'infection'.

Once here, The Health Service took over, believing that many operations, physiotherapy, artificial aids and all the segregation that goes with it, would greatly improve her life. Her own memory, from the age of seven, was of being so terrified by the new language and customs, the cold and the loss of her beloved Ayah, and the violation of her body by the surgeries that she forgot almost everything she had learned in Egypt. She came out of hospital only speaking English, the language of survival, and was put straight into 'Greenmead', an all-age special school in Tooting.

On the final day of term my Dad, not really realising what he is taking on, offers to lead both of us back to our homes in his car whilst we follow behind in our newly acquired 'Cripships'. These of course have to be brought home with us. Florence is a better driver than me, so she could have managed this journey very well were it not for the fact that she is committed to remaining in the convoy with me. I am so scared that I chug along in second gear most of the way, making the two-hour trip a four-hour ordeal. By the time we get home my Dad is an exhausted wreck, but Florence seems greatly amused by my ineptitude.

Despite our resolve to have nothing to do with 'The Disabled' ever again, we carry on being friends, growing closer and more connected as we navigate the struggle to find a place in the world together.

CHAPTER SEVENTEEN

The Shock of Reality

I AM UPSTAIRS IN my bedroom, kneeling on the floor in front of my hand-made dressing table with its' six-inch legs. My Dad had sliced them off an old coffee table. It is morning, the sun is shining through my window stirring up a strange orange glow in my golden-brown rustic-style room with hessian wallpaper. It is September 1968, late summer and the first day of Term. The house is quiet and empty as all my family have left for work.

I begin the laborious process of turning my face into Twiggy's face. Twiggy is a model whose stick thin body and dramatically painted face had been admiringly sellotaped to my wall alongside pictures of John Lennon and Bob Dylan for many months. The brown curves above the eye-lids are not too difficult, but the extra painted-on eyelashes below the eyes are a different matter as the angles have to be just right to avoid looking like Daffy Duck. I choose a fine brush and a liner which requires just the right amount of spit for the consistency I need. I delicately apply the six little lines that will make me beautiful. You have to be a proper artist to get it right and, as from today, I am going to be one.

The clock ticks away as I create my image. I am going to be late for my first day at Art College but then I am late for everything. The life I want to live holds so many fears for me that it takes ages to build up the courage to open the door and set off, but no-one would have guessed this, not even me. I just suddenly become aware of several enormously important things which have to be done before I can leave, none of which I have noticed until five minutes ago, like the pressing need to look like Twiggy and not 'Mickey'. Mickey was the nickname I had been called by my family since childhood, supposedly a shortened form of Micheline. It was not my real name and as far as I am concerned, it had been given to a version of me which existed in their heads, not mine. Mickey is a Mouse. Who am I?

Finally, I have created the right facial image befitting the beginning of this new stage of my life. I am upstairs so still have to crawl around the floor without the aid of a wheelchair. Even my specially made elbow crutches are not enough to help me get up the steep and curved staircase which don't have a banister all the way up. Tearing myself away from the pile of tangled clothes on the carpet which suddenly look like they need to be folded and put away, I go downstairs to the front door where I had placed my bag of delights the night before. The bag was a hold-all made of strong clear plastic with day-glo flowers printed all over it. Inside were those precious tools of my new trade - Stanley knife, Cow Gum, steel rule, pencil set with proper sharpeners, a Rotring drawing pen with various sized nibs. This expensive pen was the visible evidence that I intended to draw my way to freedom from the chains of my disability. I stand up with my crutches, pick up my toolkit, and with equal measures of optimism and terror open the front door to climb into my little vehicle standing in the fire-station yard outside. I coax my tiny green three-wheeled 'Baratt' invalid tricycle into sputtering smelly life, kick it into gear and roar off to tackle Sanderstead Hill (downwards) and the road to Croydon Art College. Taking my place in a mainstream Art college, alongside the new cohort of non-disabled 'normal' young people was not what I had been led to believe was my fate.

Normal People don't Exist

Art college doesn't turn out quite as I had thought. To begin with I don't know how to talk to non-disabled people and, quite frankly most of them don't know how to talk to me. I have flown in a rocket from Special Land into Normal Land with no preparation. I quickly realise that the fascinating topics of conversation I had enjoyed with my school mates, such as Miss Barley's weird hair-do, held no interest whatsoever for 'Mills-on-Wheels' whose main enthusiasm was his motor-scooter. I feel I have no opinions on anything relevant to this new environment so I decide, wisely I think, to develop instead the art of listening and asking endless questions. After all I have a lot to learn.

Luckily this turns out to be a very good strategy as I find most people like nothing better than talking about themselves. However, this takes a monumental amount of courage and energy because if I don't insert myself into groups and conversations, I will just be ignored, as if I was still in Special Land. This takes so much of my attention and energy that there was little left for learning about Art, or anything else for the whole of my Foundation Year. I do almost no work of any merit at college. I have to go home and sit up half the night to do that. College is the place where I smoke too many Number 6, listen endlessly to 'Hey Jude' on the canteen Juke Box, eat plates and plates of cheap chips and listen, listen, listen.

What I hear makes me completely re-evaluate my concept of 'normal' people. Compared to the friends I had left behind in Treloars, so many of the young people around me here seem lost, confused, inexperienced and yet to develop much wisdom of their own. They are struggling to make sense of the world just as much as I am. They are not better than me after all! It has all been a ruse, a myth made up to justify the form of apartheid so many of us have suffered.

Croydon Art College is not very high on the hierarchy of where to study art. 'The Slade' and 'Chelsea' are the places to go if you really want to get good training in your field. Our college is also a technical college. There were two quite separate groups of students queuing up at either end of the serving hatches in the canteen. One was full of slightly scruffy students in dull jeans and leather jackets whilst the other was bright and colourful - mostly wealthier students competing for the most original hair/make up/ outfits they could invent. It does not appear that these separate groups talk to each other or even sense they are in the same college. I am amazed by this. I don't really feel I belong to either group.

I do make a 'best friend', Heather who seems as much an 'outsider' as I feel, although she is tall and willowy and not disabled at all. She is not a happy person, so finding my listening ear is therapeutic for her. It is not a one-way relationship though – we laugh and talk about all manner of things until the canteen around us empties and the janitors come around to stack up the tables and turn off the lights. They ask if we don't have a home to go to, but sometimes we stay there in the half-light, smoking and putting the world to rights for a long time afterwards.

Although I am not really fulfilling my intention to become a skilled and outstanding artist by doing much work, I do enjoy the opportunity offered in the foundation year to have a go at things. I love silk-screen printing and I enjoy pottery, especially having a go at the wheel and flirting with the very handsome blue-eyed tutor.

face-painting for college

I still like 'fiddly' so I enjoy the print shop where we set up by hand lines of metal letters, spaces and punctuation marks in a wooden block and then use a huge machine to print them, which amazingly I am strong enough to operate. I vaguely understand that if we are to be designers or illustrators it is useful to understand the methods by which our work will be reproduced as it affects how we need to approach the task. Some colour work for example has to be separated out into single-colour components which are then printed over each other until the full colour design is complete.

These technological demands of reproduction all seem so limiting to me. As a would-be illustrator I began to understand that black and white line drawings had to be done in black ink because pencil is multi-tones of grey and therefore requires a more sophisticated, and expensive, printing process. The use of colour is even more dependent on the money available for the project, again because of the processes involved in its' printing. It is nothing like doing a beautiful one-off painting to hang on the wall, which is why Art books, using the most expensive forms of printing necessary to reproduce such paintings, cost a small fortune. This is why people like us don't have them in our houses, even less the paintings themselves.

Workwise, things don't really improve. After my foundation year when I choose the 'Graphic Illustration' option, I am sent to an annexe in Penge to study for my Diploma in Art and Design. There I spend far too much time laughing at the antics of my study group who quickly find I am a trapped audience for their clowning around. I am trapped because my new studio is upstairs where even the stool upon which I have to sit is shoulder-high to me, requiring one of my fellow students, Clifford, to lift me onto it, and then take me off it later, if he remembers.

The attitude the staff take towards me is that if I want to make it in the highly competitive world of Graphic Design, I will have to be twice as good any everyone else. They tell me this very seriously. No allowances will be made for me, not even a lower table and stool. I do not question them, but gradually I begin to question myself as to whether this is really a fight I want to have.

Having been brought up all my life to think that non-disabled people are better than disabled people, I am truly shocked at how these 'superior' beings actually behave. Two definitive events stand out:

The first is a student stealing a portfolio off one of our class mates in order to pass it off as his in an interview. This almost seems to be condoned by the tutors who are well aware of it, but to me it is unimaginably deceitful, especially when the real artist is supposed to be a mate.

Another is when a Tutor from another group who were taking an exam, enters my studio where I am stranded on my stool whilst everyone else is downstairs in the canteen. He is carrying a sheet of paper upon which he asks me to draw a girl doing something – I forget what. He says "Oh, my student cannot draw figures. You are so much better than her" ie "Can you help her cheat?" Do I want to spend the rest of my life working with people whose values seem so different to mine?

Apart from growing disillusionment with my new peer group, I have another problem. I don't seem to care about having a lot of money. Doing something just to make some money just doesn't motivate me at all. I don't think I really understood until then that 'Commercial Art' was not real Art at all. Real Art to me is making an internal thought or image of my own visible through the medium of paint, ink or pencil. It is a form of self-expression. What I am being taught to do at College is to sell my skills to be exploited by publishers and advertisers to make them money. I am drawing/painting their ideas, not my own. Of course, if I am successful at this I could indeed earn something for myself, but to me, the reward of having something to spend in the shops just couldn't make up for the cost of spending so much time doing something which would bring me no satisfaction at all.

I do not want to be a famous artist either. In fact, I have a deficit where ambition should have been. Is this because I have been excluded from the school system and its' values for most of my developing life? Is it because my family have instilled in me the idea that I would be 'looked after' whatever I did or didn't do? Or is it something more to do with developing a political identity of my own...

Another Road

After two years, I realize that not only am I never going to be twice as good as everyone else, I am on the wrong path for me. Without talking about it to anyone, including my parents, I pack up my Rotring Pens and tins of Cow Gum and leave with no qualifications and not a first clue as to what I am going to do instead.

In some ways I feel very sad about this. I feel my heart and soul is that of an Artist. It has been the thing which had brought me the greatest joy, but the searing shock of the real world as it is makes me feel that there is a more urgent direction to focus for my time and energy whatever my own desires are. I feel I am compelled to challenge the misinformation and discrimination which is still entrapping me and my people (Disabled People) into tiny shrunken worlds even though we have begun to escape from the actual walls of our institutional prisons. It can be likened to setting out on a journey towards a destination of my own choosing, following the main highway, obeying all the road-signs, only to find my way blocked by a huge and unexpected tangle of fallen branches and brushwood. I really have no choice at all. I have to tackle the barriers to my progress before I can press on.

AFTERWORDS

LOOKING BACK OVER THE seventy years of my life it is clear that the huge pile of brushwood became the focus of much of my attention and desire for change. It was, and is, full of what I experienced as 'Stupid Adults' although, having become one myself, I now realise that '*Stupified* Adults' is a much better description of us - stupified by misinformation, distress and an oppressive society which fuels it all.

I am proud to have rolled up my sleeves and got to work on the problem, even though it was not my first choice of labour. I had been brought up with the values of public service – socialism - so it was always apparent to me that what I did was not just for me. Although I was given a pretty heavy message as a child that my services were not wanted or needed by society, somehow, I never believed it. When the white-coated professionals turned out to be so wrong about my potential for life, and my parents decided to ignore them, think for themselves and give me a chance, I had been shown that it is best to learn from reality - by experimentation and reflection, by listening to the widest possible diversity of experience and wisdom, and to trust my own judgement, to correct my own mistakes.

So many of the fears which shaped my over-protected and isolated childhood turned out to be unfounded. They were no more that the projections of past experiences of distressed and misinformed people into the future they imagined for me.

Once out in the world I was able to learn from real people as well as books. I sought out the women's movement, joined the 'Alternative society', helped found the Disability Movement, became a teacher of co-counselling and began leading workshops around the world.

At the age of thirty-two I had a child who also has Osteogenesis Imperfecta. I was determined to become her ally through building the movement for Inclusive Education, bringing the voice of the 'excluded' into the decision-making process for the first time. I also supported parents of disabled children in the ways I wish had been available for my parents. This in turn inspired them to become allies to their children and the disability movement as a whole. Together we changed the law around the exclusion of children with 'special needs' from mainstream schools (although there is still a long way to go on this).

I travelled to many different countries, earning my way there through skills I had picked up as a trainer and public speaker. As well as being there to work, I got to see the mountains and lakes of Vancouver; gazed up at the giant redwood forests of California; touched the Little Mermaid in Denmark; bathed outside in the hot-water springs of Japan; swam 'wild' in a lake in Ontario, got splashed by the Niagra Falls, sweltered amongst the marble statues in Rome; swung above the Pyrenes in a cable car; saw fireflies in Oklahoma; and drove through the Black Forest in Germany.

I wrote and had published articles, chapters for other people's books, whole books of my own, and got to air my views several times on television and radio. Without intending to I became 'known' in the field of disability rights and inclusion. I am happy that I have tried my best to right the wrongs I saw.

But now, with hindsight, I do not think it is these achievements, important though they are, that have given my life meaning. I believe the most wonderful thing about my life has been meeting the people in it.

A few years ago I was contacted by a nurse who had looked after me during those bleak years of my very early life in Kingston Hospital. Having seen my unusual name on a book jacket she found my address and sent me a letter. In it she told me stories of how I would wait quietly for the God-Doctor to reach my cot, followed by his entourage of lowly staff, only to pull off my nappy at the last minute so he was faced by my little pink naked bum, to the horror - and delight - of the nurses, giggling behind his back. This human connection with strangers is the redeeming element of those painful episodes in my early life. Without the love of those women, I would have faded and shrunk. I would not have been playing the great nappy trick as my first political protest against white-coated authority. I would have given up. She confirmed to me that the love was two-way. It is such moments when human to human contact has been made, and we are all able to unfold a little more of our selves, that I remember with the greatest joy and sense of fulfilment.

Despite the early isolation, or perhaps because of it, I have been hungry to touch and be touched by people with as little pretence as possible. I have avoided 'partying' and been drawn instead to intimate connections with just one or two people at a time. Learning to listen early did me no harm at all because I could make people feel safe enough that they would become more real, more vulnerable, more exquisite. This is never a one-way thing. Every connection added something to me, developed an idea, an emotion, an insight or helped some learning to happen. Unshared pain is what 'stupifies' us. Connection is the healer – the melting of hurt into insight.

Every day I remember someone who emotionally touched me although many are no longer living. Not only my mental memory banks, but also my physical walls, albums, screen saver and scrap books are filled with the faces of the people to whom I have been fortune enough to get close. My family, my childhood friends, my fellow campaigners and collaborators, my colleagues at work, my wonderful daughter, many co-counselling partners, even one or two lovers – all have helped me to continue to grow into my full self. In return I have been allowed to help them become their full selves. I have come to think that this is the deep meaning of inclusion, the whole point. Conversely, the result of any form of separation or segregation actively prevents such connections. In effect they prune us like pollarded willows so our true shape can never be seen, and consequently the whole world is diminished.

So, what next? As I grow older my connection not just with people, but with the natural world seems to be growing more intense. I was born loving the roaring poplar trees, the clattering waterfalls, the bluebell woods, rain on my face and the friendly sparrows pecking around my feet. As a sullen teenager, depressed by my fears of the future, I found comfort in trees which I pressed myself against, feeling their long existence give balance to current madness.

Although I lost focus on this as I was growing up, having more pressing issues to deal with - like getting a life - when my Dad died (young, just as he had predicted) and I had a baby to raise, I built my own garden using all the knowledge he had taught me. This garden is still one of my greatest pleasures to sit in, plant and sow, weed and feed, photograph and paint.

Never before have I felt that all the unbelievable beauty of the natural world is being threatened so dangerously. The Climate Emergency and the loss of habitat for irreplaceable species now feels of the utmost urgency

I have learned that it is not more information we need. We need to be listened to whilst we process the tons of data we already have in our heads, or at our fingertips. We need to re-learn how to use our imaginations to create the world we all want. I don't have many years left, so working out what is the best thing to do to help build resistance in all its' forms, is constantly on my mind, and plans are being made...

If you want to learn more please go to my website www.michelinemason.co.uk

Printed in Great Britain
by Amazon